What About Church?
- Guidelines for Fellowship for the Home Schooling Family and the Home Church Alternative -

Jeff Barth

Parable Publishing House

 # Contents

What About Church?

- Guidelines for Fellowship
for the Home Schooling Family
and the Home Church Alternative -

Chapter One

A More Important Basis for Unity

I recently received a letter from a home schooling father in the northwestern United States. He confided that even though his family was from a town that was in the *Guiness Book of World Records* for having the most churches per capita of any city in the world, they could not find a church setting where they felt at home, one that was supportive of and a strengthening to their family-oriented, Christian values. In recent months, I have encountered many home schooling parents who are raising similar concerns.

At home schooling conventions and seminars, one question that I find frequently asked is on this issue of church involvement, and where the home schooler fits in. Not too long ago, a home schooling father of a large family in the South called one evening and was expressing satisfaction and praise for everything home schooling and Biblical child rearing had meant to his family. He went on to say, "There's only one thing I'd like to ask you, Jeff...What do you do about church?" He sensed it was causing trouble for his home. I went on to explain that he certainly wasn't alone in his sentiments, and that since we have written our book on home schooling, we have received letters and calls from home schooling fami-

lies everywhere who are asking similar questions in this area of church involvement. Many home schooling families are searching for a church setting that will give respect, support, and even praise for their family-oriented, child rearing views.

For years, Christians have been meeting together including or excluding one another on the basis of theological interpretation and denominational views (and not that these issues are unimportant), but among home schoolers, I am sensing something that goes beyond these differences; they are looking for a more important basis for unity—a basis that rests on holy and pure lifestyle, a sense of separation from the world, and Biblical child training.

In short, they are looking for a church setting that will preserve, strengthen, and enhance the Godly home; and, in general, they are willing to tolerate some differences in theology as long as this goal for the Godly home is not jeopardized. Some home schooling families have given up hope of finding such a church environment and have joined into certain church groups only to compromise their principles and convictions, and their homes have suffered for it.

The church setting plays an essential part in building a Godly home. Most home schooling families realize this; and, for this reason, the church environment is falling under careful scrutiny of the discerning, home schooling parent. Just as conscientious Christian parents in the early '70s began to question both the spiritual and character impact Christian schools were having on their children in spite of the fact they were labeled "Christian", even so today home schooling parents are beginning to look deeper and more thoughtfully and wisely at the impact the church environment is having on their home. This book is designed to give those parents some guidelines and options in making such an evaluation.

- Some General Concerns -

At the outset, what are some general concerns that should be considered by home schoolers in regards to this

issue of church involvement? First of all, keep in mind that the church will probably have the greatest social impact of any single element upon your family. Children (and parents as well) learn far more from the example they see in others rather than words of instruction. Therefore the greatest teaching conveyed through any church environment will be through the social interaction with others.

Just as children conform to the peer pressure found in a classroom, families will find they are conforming to some degree to the peer influence of their church environment. When a home schooling family tries to adjust their standards or overlook certain character concerns displayed in a church where many or most of those in attendance either church school or public school their children, there is almost always a degree of conforming that takes place in the home schooling family's lifestyle. Before long, the home schooling family finds itself adjusting its standards to "fit in", or they face some belittling or perhaps some rejection by others. Generally those who want to feel comfortable with sending their children away from home for education will tend to make light of our home-oriented convictions. So now we end up trying to prove that our methods are better, or we find ourselves trying to measure up to some ideal or supernatural standard set by such peers.

If, however, on the other hand we could have a church where the core nucleus of families were home schoolers who shared similar views on home schooling, Godly child training, and other Biblical family principles, those who came into the group would be positively influenced to adjust their standards to reach ours. God intended for the church to be this kind of example within the world.

For example, we have a small, home church meeting comprised of a nucleus of a few home schooling families who share similar convictions with us. We had another young couple begin to attend some of our meetings a while back, and before long the wife (after observing the ladies in our group) began to ask some questions about her own lifestyle.

She wanted to know if it was right for her to be working outside the home; she explained that her husband thought they needed the extra money, but she had noticed that none of the ladies in our group had jobs. We put her under grace and encouraged her to honor her husband's wishes while the older ladies in our group began to explain that a woman's role can be most rewarding at home (especially when the mother has young children-which this woman had). After a few weeks and with nothing more said by us, the husband along with his wife decided his wife would give up her job so she could stay at home with their children. At the same time this young mother began to notice a modesty in the other ladies' apparel in our group, and she began to make changes in this area of her life as well.

Peer influence can be positive or negative. We can adjust our standards to "fit in" with a certain group where we may find our family "peer pressured or peer influenced" by the practices and lifestyle of that group, or we can set a new standard by assembling with those of similar convictions and thus challenge or elevate the standards of others.

Sometimes we don't have to start a new church nucleus to do this, and there are times when the Lord may want us to "work" to change things in an established church setting. I believe there are times when God would lead a home schooling family to try to minister within an established church. There have been times when, as a family, we felt led to minister within a certain church group, and I think the Lord used our efforts. But we have found that it is very important for the home schooling family to carefully "consider themselves", taking into consideration the age of their children when attempting such a ministry. "Brethren, if a man be overtaken in a fault, ye which are spiritual restore such a one in the spirit of meekness; considering thyself, lest ye (or your children) also be tempted." (Galatians 6:1.)

In such involvements, many subtle difficulties sometimes cross our lives, and we do not recognize such temptations until we start facing struggles with our children. I know of some

home schooling families and have heard of others who attempted to minister by fitting into a certain church group only to be faced with very trying problems with their young people in the teen years. Many times we don't recognize the temptations our children are facing until it's too late; this is only one of the problems with mixing with a group that has some different standards than our own.

So my suggestion would be for the parents to carefully consider *their own children*, and if you are noticing your children's character or attitudes being negatively affected or altered by the regular, social involvement in a church, to withdraw for a while in order to rebuild the strength and character of your own home. There are priorities in Christian love, and there are many temptations that we as parents can bear but our children can not. Romans 14 talks about the importance of keeping from placing stumbling blocks in our brother's or sister's path; how much more then would this apply to our own children? It is important for parents to consider the weakest and most vulnerable one in the family when evaluating social involvements, and to curtail such involvements to accommodate this weaker vessel.

- Some Common Concerns With Church Involvement -

The first area I have had several parents express concern over is the age-segregated Sunday School and the exposures their children have in this environment away from parental supervision. One home schooling father of eight children said he had begun to think that maybe Sunday School would be all right for his children. He and his wife had just kept their children with them in worship service up to this point and had avoided Sunday School. So they began sending their children to Sunday School for a few Sundays. Then one Sunday morning, this father's little daughter (age 6 or 7) took her father by the hand and said, "Daddy, I need you to go to Sunday School with me today." He sensed his little girl had some concerns with the class so he went along with her.

He said he was shocked with the things he was unaware that

his daughter was facing, the aggression, teasing, and mischief. This wise little girl wanted to be sure that her father would approve of what she was involved with. Since her father was a loving disciplinarian in the home, she sensed he would not feel good about the behavior of the children in the classroom, and her conscience was bothering her. The father told me, "It was a real eye opener to me."

Because of similar situations, many home schooling families opt out of Sunday School. Many churches are becoming sensitive to this concern of parents with the elementary age Sunday School class and are substituting a little children's message at the start of the regular worship service. This is one alternative, but we would suggest that children remain beside the parents while the children's message is brought. Sometimes children's church can pull children away from parents, too. Staying in close proximity with parents during church helps children stay under proper authority.

Many parents do not like the idea of having to put their babies in the nursery or toddlers' class, and many churches are accommodating these concerned parents, but some churches feel this is a disruption with having little ones in the service. We have found that with a reasonable amount of training, children can be taught to sit rather quietly through a service. The best training for this is having the children sit quietly on a regular basis through family devotions at home, or sit quietly on mother's or father's lap during a story time, etc. Have a time of teaching and singing, and work with the young children until they will sit quietly at mother's or father's requests. This may require some spankings and persistent training from parents throughout the week.

Some parents express the concern that other parents do not supervise and control their own children during church or following church during fellowship time. This was a concern with one church that we attended for a while, and we talked to the leadership about this. One of the elders shortly after that began announcing at the close of the service that parents should supervise and control their own children during the

fellowship following the service.

Another home schooling parent expressed concern with the conversations her twelve year old daughter was facing during the fellowship time. The mother knew that her daughter was being exposed weekly to the companionship of other young girls who were public schooled and private schooled, and she was worried about the values, lifestyle, attitudes, and other temptations her daughter was faced with. The mother said to my wife, "I felt like I was sending my daughter to public school with all the negative exposure she was getting." They began attending our small home fellowship. A lot of the child discipline problems home schoolers face through the week can be traced back to wrong peer influence at church. This is an area to consider if you are facing some frustrations with child discipline.

Often the concern is with the teen influence. If teens generally segregate among themselves or separate from the rest of their family, this is an indication that they will be presenting other so-called "freedoms" to your teens that you would rather your teens weren't confronted or tempted with; and, of course, your teen cannot help but to begin to question some of your more restrictive principles.

Some parents have expressed concern with preaching or discussions raised on subjects which lacked the purity they wished it would have had for their children to hear; at least it seemed to be inappropriate for a holy, church setting. They had the feeling that their children's minds were being exposed to areas where it seemed they should remain innocent and pure.

Now to face these situations once in a while does not bring a family down too much, but sitting in this kind of a church environment week after week for a long period of time will eventually erode a home schooling family's standards or else cause them to become less sensitive or discerning as to what are the best ways for the Godly home. Furthermore, because we have lowered our standards to fit into theirs they begin to reason that we are just like them, and so our ministry

becomes less effective. The "salt" loses its savor. (Matthew 5:13.)

If, however, the home schooling family does choose to attend an organized church of some kind where they may be getting some of this exposure, I would suggest finding a smaller assembly or group. Generally the larger churches are able to offer more programming and activities which tend to not only tempt our children, but also separate our families. Early church history indicates that believers in the first few centuries met together only one day a week where there was reading of the apostles' doctrine, preaching, teaching, singing, and sometimes the sharing of a meal. (Henry Sheldon's *History of the Christian Church,* Vol. 1, pp. 278, 279.) This arrangement allowed for more than ample family time throughout the week to build and maintain family unity and principles. Modern church programming has deviated from the early church example, causing what some feel is a weakening to the structure of the home due to too much socializing and inadequate family time.

Someone may raise the question, "What should we do if after attending a church for a while we do not seem to meet another family that is interested in our ways? Should we continue to attend?" Here again you will need to wisely consider how the involvement is impacting your family. There have been times in the past when as a family we have been a part of an organized church when it seemed that no one was being "drawn" to us, and if we found the church influence to be affecting our lifestyle too heavily, we would withdraw for a while to rebuild our family unity and strength. We all want to help others, but none of us can afford to do this at the expense of our own children.

I realize there are some home schooling families who think they should try to help others or fit in, regardless of the impact on their own home, reasoning that God will give them grace to stand. Far too often I have seen tragic results happen to home schooling teens whose parents thought they were ministering as a family in a particular church.

Years ago when the home schooling movement began, we

found similar arguments from those who insisted we should first of all attempt to mend the problems with the church schools or Christian schools rather than to be so radical as to home school. But none of us early home schooling parents were against education or learning; we were just discovering a more effective, Godly way and atmosphere in which to do it. I believe we are making similar discoveries with the church system as we traditionally know it. None of us are against assembling—we just want to be able to assemble in a way which will protect and enhance and build the Godly home.

We must be very careful as to what we are "getting" from certain church situations. Most of us home schooling parents have heard the similar argument that we should be placing our children in public schools so that they can learn to be "missionaries" there, a witness for the Lord; and as home schoolers know, there have been many a Christian family victimized by that philosophy. Am I saying that as home schoolers we should never attend a church that does not support our views? I am not necessarily saying that, but husbands and wives together with a blended conscience and discernment should carefully consider the long range impact of their church involvement on their marriage and family life. Many of the struggles of the home can be traced back and contributed to the church involvement of that family. Wisely and vigilantly consider this.

With over seventeen years of home schooling experience, we have had many opportunities to meet many home schooling families. Those who faced struggles with their teens have primarily faced these difficulties because they did not carefully consider the social, philosophical, and lifestyle influence the church was having on their home. Some of these families acknowledged that they could sense the church environment was adversely affecting their family, but because the church tradition as we know it in America today is held up as so sacred and not to be questioned, they simply went along with the status quo of things only to face struggles years later within their own home.

In the end some of them came away feeling that home schooling had let them down, and many of their Christian friends ended up scoffing at the value of home schooling, when sadly home schooling was not the real root cause of the problem. Most home schooling parents have carefully evaluated over the years the impact the school systems would have on their children and home life. This process of evaluation doesn't end when we bring our children home; it must be continued as we carefully evaluate every source that will ultimately affect our home. This evaluation is often done through trial and error, trying something and then evaluating the effect on our lives. The mature Christian has learned to do this, and the wise parent will foresee the evil and avoid it.

- Nehemiah & Ezra -

When Ezra and Nehemiah set out to rebuild the temple and walls of Jerusalem so that worship could be restored to the people of God, it is interesting to observe how the unity of the family was retained during the process. The work was apportioned to individual families laboring together on different projects; and when it was necessary to take defensive measures, this too was by individual families.

"Therefore, set I in the lower places behind the wall, and on the higher places, I even set the people *after their families* with their swords, their spears, and their bows. And I looked, and rose up, and said unto the nobles, and to the rulers, and to the rest of the people, Be not ye afraid of them; remember the Lord, which is great and terrible, and fight for your brethren, your sons, and your daughters, your wives, and your houses." (Nehemiah 4:13,14.)

God wants to restore worship to the people of God today, but He wants to do it in a way that will protect the unity and integrity of the home. God never intended for man to build one institution at the expense of another. The church and the home are to support each other. Far too often today, building the church has become a substitute for building up the families that make it up.

- A New Trend In Assembling -

In recent months we are witnessing new church settings arising—church assemblies made up, in general, of a nucleus of home schooling families who are attempting to establish a core group foundation to their assembly and who have set the Godly home as the basis for their unity. We have noticed many families in these churches coming together with different theological backgrounds and idealisms, but they are getting along well because they have this one central goal of building the Godly home as their most important basis for unity. Some of these groups are meeting in homes, and some have grown into larger assemblies that the home will no longer accommodate.

The leadership in these groups is being shared somewhat cooperatively by the fathers in the group who seem to display the most spiritual maturity. (Qualifications for church leadership are discussed in more detail in a later chapter.) I believe we are seeing a re-emergence of the church similarly to the way it was in those New Testament days, and let us bear in mind that the greatest expansion the church has ever experienced in history was in those first few centuries where believers, for the most part, met in homes and other smaller assemblies.

In this book I want to explore some Biblical church options. For those who feel the call to minister as a family in an established or traditional church environment, the information in these pages will present some objectives and challenges for such a ministry. For those families who, for one reason or another, feel the challenges of a ministry in the traditional church setting to be beyond their present considerations, we offer the option of the home church or something similar.

I will avoid specifying what size the church should be or what kind of building in which to meet. For some, the home will seem very adequate; for others some kind of meeting hall or church building would be the preference. Although most of the N.T. churches were thought to be house churches, this is not necessarily a "must" or a Biblical precedent set

down. Paul met in the school of one Tyrannus with some disciples for two years. (Acts 19:9,10.)

In the N.T., we have a fair description of what these churches were like and how authority structure was set up in them. Many large churches today, even denominations, started out as a small group meeting in someone's house. So when I use the term *house church* in this book, it should be understood that at some point some groups may find it necessary to seek a larger facility. But in the following chapters, I would like to explore some of the advantages of the smaller assembly and give further suggestions for this important area of the assembling of believers.

Chapter Two

The Home Church—A Biblical Option

I am observing a growing trend among Christians towards this idea of starting a home-oriented type of church meeting. Generally it is the home schooling parent who is particularly interested in the idea, and this may stem from several reasons. But perhaps one of the main reasons is that home schoolers have already broken out of the traditional group or an organization-minded, educational system and have discovered a more effective method at home. Thus they are not afraid to question traditions and to reinitiate some earlier methods.

Although the home church may be less commonly found in America at present, it is certainly not a new idea in history, and in some countries like Communist China it plays a major part in Christian assembly today. In fact, the only churches which are addressed in Paul's letters were probably almost exclusively home churches, and for the first two to three hundred years of the early church, they were predominantly home churches.

In Acts, Chapter 4, we do find that the Jerusalem church had grown into a congregation of at least five thousand members. This was definitely not a house church. Even with twelve apostles, they were not able to meet the needs of this large group. In the sixth chapter of Acts, we see that they selected seven other men to help care for the needs. These additional men not only looked after the widows and similar duties, but were very spiritual men who were later involved in preaching, evangelistic ministry, and in church planting. So there were no less than nineteen men in leadership.

One would think that God would allow such a large group of believers as this one in Jerusalem to remain intact. Those of us in America would certainly think such an impressive organization would carry an influence that God would be able to greatly use. However, we find in Acts, Chapter 8, Verse 1, that there was to arise a "great persecution against the church which was at Jerusalem"; and in Verse 4 of this chapter, we discover God's reason for allowing this persecution—"Therefore, they that were scattered abroad went everywhere preaching the Word." The Gospel was greatly expanded, and many, new, Christian works sprang as a result of this persecution.

From this point on in the book of Acts, we see a definite trend towards the smaller assembly, and not until the close of the third century do we find a shift from these methods. At the time of Christ and early apostles, synagogues were common, but we do not find any instances where Jesus or the early apostles suggested the construction of such structures for meeting places for Christians (not that some house churches which had outgrown the practicality of meeting in a home were prohibited from meeting in a larger facility—this just wasn't a common occurrence.)

Paul frequently addresses churches in homes and commends households who had made their homes into centers for Christian ministry. (See Romans 16:5; Colossians 4:15; Philemon vs 2; and Acts 2:46, 5:42, and 20:20.) Granted, there were periods of persecution against the believers in these early days of the church which may account for the tendency at times for a less

visible means of assembly that the house church affords; but perhaps (and I think probably more so) God allowed this persecution to continue in order to preserve the distinct advantages of the smaller church assembly.

- The House Church Through History and Today -

For years we Christians in America have been praying for revival in our land. It was interesting to me that when studying past revivals in history, it is discovered that home type of assemblies or smaller groups many times played an important part in the initial stages of revival. New spiritual ideals often began in small pockets or cell groups of Christians who wanted to break out of the mold that often held Christians in complacency.

During the Great Awakening of the early 1700's and the revival in Europe, Philip Spener of Frankfurt, Germany, was a central figure. "He wanted to recover Luther's appeal to the heart and set up *house meetings* for prayer, Bible study, and the sharing of Christian experience." (From *Eerdman's Handbook to the History of Christianity*, p. 442.) Note how these meetings allowed for the attendance to personal spiritual concerns and interaction among believers.

Around this same time, "James Hutton became the first English member of the Moravian church, and was to play a leading role in the English Revival. *In his house* met the religious society from which both the Moravian and the Methodist witness in England sprang. Other similar groups soon appeared, some of which attracted German exiles." (From *Eerdman's Handbook*, p. 444.)

John and Charles Wesley's "Holiness Club" started out as a small group of men who wanted to meet together to share personal Christian experience and spiritual insight. They were striving to have a more intimate spiritual experience with other Christians and to pray for one another's needs. "John Wesley traced the 'first rise' of Methodism to these years." (*Eerdman's Handbook*, p. 450.) "It was in this same small assembly (the Holiness Club) where Charles Wesley guided the devo-

tional reading of George Whitefield before his conversion." (*Eerdman's Handbook*, p. 447.) Two of the greatest revivalists in the history of the church, John Wesley and George Whitefield, credited the foundation of their spiritual experience to a small Christian cell group.

Similarly, our Pilgrim fathers actually started out as a small Separatist group that had broken away from the Church of England. They started out as "a group of Puritans who met for prayer and discussion *at the house* of William Brewster in the nearby village of Scrooby" in Nottinghamshire, England. (From *Of Plymouth Plantation* by William Bradford.) The Pilgrims were not actually Puritans as such; they were more accurately Separatists. Many of the Puritans remained with the Church of England and hoped to purify it. Other Puritans, dubbed Separatists, withdrew from the Church of England and formed their own churches. William Bradford was only in his teen years when he began meeting with this group at Brewster's house. Most of these groups faced much persecution and belittling; it is said in Cotton Mather's biography of Bradford that Bradford joined Brewster's group despite "the wrath of his uncles" and the "scoff of his neighbors".

It is interesting to note that the major concerns that the Puritans and the Separatists had with the established Church of England in their day are very similar to the major concerns that home schooling parents are having with the established churches in America. First, the Puritans were wanting to see more purity within the church (that's why they were mockingly called Puritans), and they wanted to "abolish the religious ceremonies" that had been passed down for years. They could sense that the church had lapsed into protecting the traditions and doctrines passed down for centuries and had lost sight of the real reason for assembling—the building of pure, separate, and Godly lives.

Secondly, they had begun to question the authority of those in leadership. They realized that the purity and principles of a church group are largely established by those in leadership, and many of the bishops in the Church of England lacked

personal discipline and were not good examples to follow.

Thirdly, they became more aware of the effects of socialization on their families (this is part of purifying). Bradford writes that this was one of their concerns which actually helped prompt them to make their decision to move from Holland to the New World. "But that which was more lamentable, and of all sorrows most heavy to be borne, was that many of their children, by these occasions and the great licentiousness of youth in that country, (Holland) and the manifold temptations of the place, were drawn away by evil examples into extravagant and dangerous courses, getting the reins off their necks (out from under parental authority) and departing from their parents." (From *Of Plymouth Plantation* by William Bradford.)

Research shows that the Pilgrim church in Holland before they embarked to New England had grown to a sizable number of between four and five hundred members (some historians place the number of members as high as 1,000) of which only approximately one hundred journeyed to America. Bradford said this about their church system, "It was shapen much nearer the first Christian churches, as it was used in the apostles' times."

-Tremendous Expansion of the Early Church-

Actually perhaps the greatest expansion that Christianity has ever experienced was in those first two to three hundred years after Christ, and this was predominantly accomplished through the instrument of the house church and smaller assemblies. Around the year 313 A.D., freedom of religion or more precisely freedom of Christianity became more common after Constantine's Edict of Milan. At the time of the edict, the "basilica style of church (a building where large congregations met) seems rapidly to have replaced the house church." (From *Eerdman's Handbook*, p. 150.)

About this same time, moral decline began to permeate the Roman Empire. I believe this moral decline was at least, in part, caused by the parallel decline that was also beginning to take

place within the church. What brought about this moral decline within the church?

Previously the house churches had allowed for an intimate attendance to the needs of each Christian's life and family. Each member sought and prayed diligently for scriptural answers to the struggles of others. There was a sense of mutual edification in the house churches. However, with the larger congregations now meeting in the basilicas, this intimacy among brethren was beginning to be lost. Problems were dealt with inadequately or left unaddressed if they were raised at all; thus Godliness and holiness were jeopardized. The house churches also provided more of a sense of separation from the world and its idolatry; but now that Christianity had been more popularized by the Edict of Milan, it wasn't uncommon to find those with less commitment to Godliness attending the meetings. "The house church had usually provided enough room for the persecuted Christian. Now that Christianity was respectable and officially recognized, the numbers of worshipers increased rapidly." (*Eerdman's Handbook,* pp. 150, 151.) Soon it was not too uncommon to find nominal Christians attending the services and presenting their lifestyle to all of those present just as it is in most larger churches today in America.

The basilica type church meeting also created a decline in qualified church leadership. Before this time, a hundred house churches would have had a total of three or four hundred leaders, each church having 2-5 leaders (who met or were striving to meet the moral and spiritual qualifications described in I Timothy 3 and Titus) and many more men working towards these qualifications. There were prophets, evangelists, and pastors and teachers who met the qualifications for leadership, ministering to the spiritual needs of the assembly.

By the consolidation of these hundreds of smaller house churches into a few, large, basilica type churches, the number of necessary leaders was drastically diminished, and the church as a whole began to experience a leadership crisis just as we have today. But more than this, since the basilicas were now looking for the most eloquent men to lead their congregation, a complacency began to set in among the common men and fathers.

-Where Are the Men?-

Today we are hearing the cry, "Where are the men in Christian leadership?"

Wives are complaining, "Why won't my husband take the spiritual lead?"

There are several causes that lie at the root of this problem: first of all, men sometimes fail to see the calling to spiritual leadership and ministry in the home, because for years we have sent our children away to other teachers and placed them under other leaders. Sunday school and youth leaders have, in many instances, also become a substitute for this role for the father.

Some recent home schooling curriculum suppliers have attempted to aid fathers and encourage fathers to take an active role of spiritual leadership and being a teacher of Biblical principles in the home. These suppliers have recognized the problem, but unfortunately when an outside supplier becomes the "source" of spiritual meat for the home rather than it coming from the father, the father doesn't learn or grow in the ability to discover or find spiritual wisdom for his own home. Wives and children soon recognize that this teaching isn't really coming from Dad, so this in time can tend to actually weaken his position of leader rather than strengthen it. Some younger fathers or newly converted fathers may find such sources of spiritual teaching helpful at first, but before long the father should be finding and presenting insight he has discovered directly from the Lord, Himself, through his personal study of the Word. Not that each husband or father wouldn't draw from a Christian brother's insight from time to time to supplement his own teaching, but just that he should not grow to be dependent on these sources.

Sometimes wives complicate things by circumventing their husband's leadership and going to others whom they would consider more spiritually gifted, talented, or wise. Wives

need to stay under their husbands in this area; they need to encourage their husbands in this area of finding and teaching spiritual insight, even if it is not so profound at first; in time your husband will be blessing you and your family with much spiritual wisdom and insight.

A second cause for this decline in spiritual leadership of men lies in our present church leadership selection, qualification, and training methods. Christian men or fathers do not see in their lives the possibility or the potential for becoming a "leader" in the church because current church leadership ordination and designation methods do not allow for this. We do not have a system in most of our churches that allows for the advancement of the father who displays spiritual growth and ability to a place of leadership. For this reason most men's spiritual gifts lay dormant or else they wither, and any desire or inclination the men may have for taking a place of leadership in the church is held in check by the present system. The motivation is lost today. Many times men are kept busy in certain responsibilities like teaching the fourth graders or a bus ministry. Keeping busy is a far cry from being able to minister our spiritual gifts and insight to the congregation at large.

This wasn't the policy of the early church. "As every man hath received the gift they were to minister these gifts one to another as good stewards of the overall or manifold grace of God." (I Peter 4:10.) Every man's spiritual gift came into play in the church (I have more to say on this in subsequent chapters), and when they chose leaders they "looked out among them" and chose men from among their ranks, men of qualification, to take a position of leadership and authority in the church. The spiritual training of future leaders was a ministry of the local church. This provided excellent motivation for men to take and work towards being spiritual leaders, not only at home but also in the church.

We have departed from this system today. Most men are expected to sit and listen rather than to be carefully learning and preparing themselves to one day minister with other men

to the spiritual needs of the assembly. We once attended for a while a church made up mostly of home schooling families. They had a shared, plural ministry in this church conducted by the men with the most spiritual maturity. The leadership was available to any man who fulfilled the qualifications (as described in I Timothy & Titus) and who desired to minister. I was amazed at how spiritually minded those men were, how knowledgeable of Scripture, how vigilant. There was no leadership crisis in that church, and there were a lot of men who could share insight and teaching. Their church system encouraged leadership qualities, and being home schooling fathers, these men were also spiritual leaders in their own homes. If, in the home schooling movement, we can go one step farther and not only give the men spiritual leadership at home (which home schooling can do), but also change our church leadership structure to allow men to take the lead or share in the lead, we will no longer hear the cry, "Where are the men in Christian leadership?"

- Intimate House Worship -

Before the Edict of Milan in 313 A.D., "...worship in the house church had been an intimate kind in which all present had taken an active part. But by the beginning of the fourth century, the distinction between clergy and lay people was becoming more prominent. About this time the liturgy (method of worship) changed from being a corporate action of the whole church into a service said by the clergy to which the laity listened." (*Eerdman's Handbook*, p. 151.)

This is exactly what we find in most every traditional church in America today; the clergy speaks, and the laity listens. The basilica churches that started around 313 A.D. succeeded in building impressive organizations, while intimacy was lost and the quality of the average Christian's spiritual life and homelife declined. But the point that is most disturbing about this centralizing of the house churches into basilica type churches is that this consolidation, along with putting the leadership of the masses of Christians into the hands of a few clergymen, actu-

ally became one of the basis by which the Roman priesthood hierarchy eventually gained its hold on the church!

Early house churches (before the Edict of Milan in 313 A.D.) divided and multiplied like cells which accounts for the early churches' rapid spreading and growth in those first few centuries. Someone might be quick to argue; yes, but didn't some of those house groups get way off on their doctrines? I would suppose so, but aren't there entire groups of Christians, even denominations, today which we would call "way off" in some way? Instead of having two small house groups of Christians differing in doctrine, we have entire denominations who blast each other as heretical! Large Christian organizations with their councils and boards which are set up to protect policy and theology have certainly not been any more successful either today in protecting soundness, and a false principle initiated at the top of a large organization has the effect of trickling down and affecting everyone under it. Whereas smaller groups due to their size and autonomy will actually help prevent this trickling down of false philosophy and principles. They will tend to protect against false doctrine being spread.

- House Churches Today -

House churching methods are not restricted to those early centuries; they are commonly found today in countries throughout the world. A current Christian newsletter reads, "In recent months many thousands are coming to Christ in Russia through the instrument of western evangelistic teams. Many of these new converts are being discipled through *house churches*. Lord willing, this will be the beginning of a major church planting effort in the Ukraine with a goal of establishing one hundred new home churches." In recent years communist China has experienced tremendous revival and growth of the Christian faith, and this has all been accomplished through *house churches*.

In 1949, the Communist Revolution took place in mainland China. At that time the Communists swept out all of the American denominational missionary groups along with their meth-

ods, leaving an estimated 70,000 Christians scattered abroad throughout China. These Christians were forced to turn underground and met in *house churches*. But in the past 40 years, this meager beginning of only 70,000 has mushroomed into an estimated 70,000,000 Christians converted to Christ; and bear in mind that this has all happened while under extreme repression and persecution. This is modern day proof that house church methods of evangelism and of building up the believer work very well. "Meanwhile, an estimated 70,000,000 Chinese have converted to Christianity since the Communist Revolution in 1949, and most worship in underground *house churches*. Recent reports reveal that over 20,000 a day are converting to Christianity." (*Report from China*, Vol II, #1, March 1991-Published by Christian Aid Mission, Charlottesville, Va.)

This is over 7,000,000 a year (some estimates indicate nearly 20,000,000 a year) currently becoming Christians in China; and because of the extreme persecution there, we can be sure that these are not just nominal Christians just wanting to call themselves Christians. Another recent report that I will leave anonymous for the protection of those believers reads this way:

Village House Churches Spreading!

In the rural areas where humble people have just enough food to survive, the believers' first dream is always to build a modest house for worship—or add a meeting room to an existing house. Not comparable with any magnificent western church building, God's "temples" in these areas are merely built of mud-bricks with straw roofs and appear to be <u>private residences</u>. Occasionally, believers can afford some real bricks for walls and tiles for roofs.

So, in these rural villages where the Communists have reluctantly loosened their controls, church buildings are springing up like bamboo shoots after the rain. This is happening from North to South and from East to West!

The Communists openly deplore the fact that they have difficulties establishing even a Communist Party school in these areas, yet these "crazy half-starving Christians" (as

they call us) are swiftly building churches in one village after another!

Similarly house church Christianity has flourished in recent decades in Eastern European countries and Korea, and has long been active in what was formerly the Soviet Union. When one considers the success of their methods under such extreme conditions and persecution, I think we American evangelicals could learn some things from them. Maybe it's time we stop exporting our church methods and begin importing some of theirs.

As a home schooling family, we have been involved in house type churches off and on for over 17 years. One house church we met with for a while had actually grown to the extent that it was no longer practical to meet in the home, so they built a separate building that would more adequately accommodate the families involved. We have become acquainted with many other house churches that were smaller than this, and were surprised to find that among these groups the percentage of young people falling away from the faith and Christian service was practically none or occurred very seldom. Furthermore, there seemed to be a zeal for the things of God among all the men, young and old, within these churches because each man saw in his life the potential for being a co-leader with others, ministering to the needs of the brethren. Wives and daughters within these groups are finding their homes as their first place of ministry as well and are also learning the joys of assisting their husbands and fathers in ministering.

I believe that we not only have ample Biblical and historical evidence but sufficient present day proof to show that house type churches are very Biblical and effective, not only for outreach but above all for preparing future Godly generations. It does take some time to adapt to it because most Christians have grown to be somewhat entertainment minded by the large church assemblies with their pomp and programming. But once families grow to appreciate the Godliness and mutual

edification that the smaller church assembly offers, much of the past tradition will seem unimportant and unproductive.

God intended the church gathering to be a meeting of brethren for the "edifying of one another in love" and "as every man had received the gift even so they were to minister one to another." Christians were to anticipate assembling together with these goals in mind. Each father ministered his spiritual gift, Biblical insight, and proven Christian experiences with others for their "good to edification." A wife's insight and spiritual wisdom were certainly not left out of the picture either. Although it is our feeling based upon Scripture that the women should be limited in their expressions (speaking) or teaching in the actual church assembly, their spiritual abilities and wisdom from God are of definite value when funneled through and discerned and appropriately expressed to the congregation by their husbands. There is tremendous value in a wife's or daughter's spiritual insight when it is kept under their proper, God-ordained authority.

We have also found the home church to be an ideal situation for the older women to instruct the younger women (young married and daughters) valuable truth from experience in the area of marriage and home life. The older women (more spiritually experienced and mature) were to teach the younger women how to love their husband (the wife's role in marriage), to love their children (the mother's role in child training), and to be discreet, chaste keepers at home—to see their home as their first ministry for Christ. (See Titus 2.)

The church setting should provide an atmosphere where wives and daughters can readily be involved in this kind of counseling ministry designated to older women. The early church relied heavily upon this ministry of women; today, however, the shift has been to allow the pastor this function of counseling younger women which is not only less effective but also opens up many men to temptations.

The church setting was to be the place where one could go to see examples of those who knew truth and were living it out in daily life...a place where successful marriages and Godly homes

are exemplified, where child training and discipline are the rule—not an after thought, and where Christians can find a refreshing, pure refuge from an evil world around them. It was and is to be therefore the "pillar and ground of the truth." With these thoughts in mind, how does one go about finding or starting such a Christian group?

Chapter Three

Finding Those of a Like-mind and Kindred Spirit

Since we have written our books on child training and Christian marriage, we have been receiving letters and hearing from families who are standing alone for the Godly home. These families are being called Remnant Families today, and they are everywhere. Let me describe a few common characteristics of these families: 1.) They generally have close marriages and are couples discerning the issues of life together. 2.) They are attending to their child training. 3.) They are trying to live a life of greater separation from worldliness. 4.) The father is the spiritual leader, teacher, and priest in his home. 5.) Wives are guiding the house and desiring to teach the younger women to serve the Lord in their own home. 6.) And, in general, they are trying to set a new standard for the Christian home.

But, unfortunately, these families seem to be scattered abroad; they don't seem to be concentrated in any particular locale in our nation. It's as if God took a handful of salt and tossed it out across our land. These families are the seed bed of a future harvest of many Godly homes, and I have a feeling that in time they will be laying the foundation of many Godly assemblies; but, right now, many are alone in their convictions.

So in setting out to find those who are of kindred spirit with you, I would not expect to find great numbers. If you find one or maybe two families in your area with similar convictions, I would say at this present time you are doing fairly well. I know of some families who are willing to travel for several hours to fellowship with another like–minded family or group (they do not meet together every Sunday). Some areas of our country are more deeply entrenched in traditional churching methods than others. So in some regions, families may find other families less ready to buck the traditions, and persecution and scorn may be more prevalent in some areas than others.

Many years ago after relocating to another state to begin home schooling, we began to consistently observe throughout the week encouraging results in our child training. However, much of this progress seemed to be offset or hindered by our church attendance at the large evangelical church we were attending at that time. So, we began trying some smaller ones, only to be faced with similar results. This period, when our children were very young, was a frustrating time for us in this area of Christian assembly.

We tried many different churches each having different meeting times. We met on Sunday morning with one group. We tried meeting with a different group for a while on Sunday evening. We tried meeting on Saturday night with some other Christians at another time, and then there were periods of time when we just had home church with just our own family.

At first we wrestled with false guilt that our upbringing and church tradition had placed upon us if we weren't in a church every Sunday morning. However, as we began to observe how fulfilled our spiritual life was even though we were meeting in a different manner and at less commonly accepted times, this guilt was soon laid aside. I usually fell back upon our home schooling example. I realized that as home schoolers we had certainly deviated from the traditional educational methods, but we could also see we were being very successful. Similarly this is what we began to notice with our churching methods. One of your biggest struggles will be with working through

some of this mis-placed guilt that tradition will sometimes evoke on our consciences.

Of course, there will be those who insist that their traditions are Biblically based, and those who are less grounded in Biblical wisdom will be more easily swayed by such persuasion. But, the fruit that we were now seeing in our home encouraged us to keep on exploring some other church options.

Evaluating church involvement is not always easy to do. Just as in every issue that affects the home, my wife and I have learned our best choices have been those that were made with a unity of spirit and a blended conscience of discernment between us. Be alert to cautious feelings either from the husband or wife. There have been times when my wife's cautious feelings helped me to avoid a church entanglement that I now know would have spelled problems for our younger ones. On the same token I can see that my concerns and cautions in other church situations also helped us to avoid some exposure that would have led to trouble for our teens or in other ways for our home.

Be careful with getting roped into certain church duties, responsibilities, or other personal commitments such as teaching a class, sitting on a board, or being put in charge of this or that. Usually about the time a home schooling family starts feeling a little uncomfortable with their church involvement, someone conveniently comes up with some such obligation or commitment to keep us tied down. The Lord has ways of making us feel uncomfortable in a church situation and ways of showing us that He has a different plan for us in this area of assembling; don't be afraid to try some different options.

One point I try to get home schooling parents to realize is this: your family and children are going to pick up the lifestyle and mannerisms of those they fellowship with to a large degree, either in church or any social involvement. One of the most important things that a parent can do in child training is to keep their child's mind and conscience innocent. When your child is little, they will pick up the attitudes and actions of others near their age. As your child approaches the teen years,

they will continue to do this; but their more mature minds will now also begin to pick up and ponder the contents of what is being taught and discussed in the church or social environment.

I remember being shocked by some of the topics discussed and illustrations used upon some of our visits to what would be considered sound evangelical churches when our children were younger. Somehow Christians have come to feel a sense of duty in bringing up so much of the perversion and iniquity from the world around us as though we parents were unaware that we are living in a corrupt perverse society. Much of this talk wounds the tender conscience of a young person and puts thoughts into their minds that will bring mental temptations to their life. It would have been so much better for your pre-teen and early teen to have never heard this. The later teen years and early twenties would be a more appropriate age to confront such discussion (and preferably in private). Carefully avoid situations where details of moral sin of the world, moral struggles of Christians, even testimonies that contain detail of moral victory are given. Particularly avoid discussions on Christian reading materials that describe or use terminology that arouses curiosity in moral areas. Teen–agers are especially vulnerable to this, and Christian radio also is often a source of this—so carefully monitor these sources.

My Bible tells me that it is "a shame to even speak of such things", let alone make them the topic of a public discussion. I finally learned my lesson after this happened a few times when my children were little, and so I began "spying out" church services by myself alone before risking exposing my wife and children to such talk and other concerns.

When my children were little, we would often go for several weeks in between before "trying" another church. Upon such visits, it seemed like invariably we would meet a family who was contemplating home schooling. We would usually invite this family over and not only encourage them in home schooling, but also begin to build a fellowship relationship with them. We know of many home schooling families who have had simi-

lar experiences with their visits to local churches.

One thing I did begin to notice when my children were young was that whenever we skipped church and had home church, our children usually enjoyed having Dad teach them. I recall an incident that happened several years ago. We had relocated to another state and had been home churching for a while until I had time enough to spy out what I hoped would be a suitable church to attend. We finally found one that even had several home schooling families involved in it. However, after visiting a few Sundays in a row, Marge and I were beginning to feel a little uncomfortable with some of the social pressures and other concerns that were being exerted upon our children. We could sense they were being drawn away, and our family unity was already beginning to be strained a little.

It was Saturday evening, and we were discussing as a family whether we thought we should go back to that church in the morning or not. My children were being very quiet (I could tell they didn't really want to go), and my then 10 year old daughter spoke up softly, "Daddy, we like it when you teach us." I remember feeling a little pleasantly surprised with her comment and the way the other children agreed with her.

I don't think as fathers we realize how much our children appreciate and enjoy it when we teach them from the Scriptures. This is particularly true if your children are not hearing Bible stories taught to them every day as a part of their curriculum. It is so much more meaningful to your children when they hear Father or Mother teach the stories, and when they see the parents draw out the specific application to life. This encourages children to look for similar applications on their own from Scripture for their own life.

We eventually began home churching more regularly. At first, we would just have a family over every week or so who shared in some of our convictions and views. I believe this was a very acceptable way in God's sight for us to assemble together at first, although we didn't necessarily meet on Sunday morning or every week. Just as school takes place wherever learning is involved, assembling takes place where two or more

Christians meet together in Jesus' name. "For where two or three are gathered together in my name, there am I in the midst of them." (Matthew 18:20.)

For years, as pioneer home schoolers, people could never quite believe we were having "school" in our home because this just did not fit into their preconceived idea of what constituted "school". The same general prejudices affect the minds of most Christians in this area of church or assembling. Of course, if we were to tell some Christian brother from China we were having "home church" in our home, they would think nothing of it; in fact, they would probably get excited. But, presently in our society, I think we are going to have to face the stigma that is sometimes a part of trying something new. But, aren't we home schoolers use to that?

- The Opposition of Tradition -

Our greatest opposition to date seems to be from Christians who are intolerant of anyone who doesn't follow the traditional American mind set of what constitutes a church. In many regards, we are like the early Reformers of the fifteenth century who came to realize that the church traditions that had been passed along from one generation to another for centuries was not really the only way of doing things, in spite of the fact that most everyone was accustomed to following those traditions.

There are also many Christian leaders today who have been schooled and operate schools in the traditional mind set. They are taught to diligently guard the traditions passed down. They seem to me a lot like the Roman priesthood that challenged the Reformers in the fifteenth century, and the school officials who challenged the home schoolers in the late 1970's. They feel a sense of duty in defending the traditions. Furthermore, because church leadership today has evolved into an occupation or source of income, instead of a God ordained position of ministry, many have a "special interest" in the traditions remaining intact. It's a lot like the teaching profession becoming alarmed at parents assuming a role of school teaching; it is a

threat to their status and livelihood. Many of them have also spent thousands of dollars and years of time acquiring their position. They are not going to readily concede that a father, trained mostly in his own home, can be just as qualified as they are.

- Finding Others For Your Church -

I don't know of any particular method which seems to work the best in finding other Christian families who are "like-minded" in this area of assembling. God's Spirit will work this out. We met one family which began meeting with us for home fellowship at a Baptist church we had visited. Another time in another area to which we had moved, we met a family when visiting another large denominational church. However, God brought us together with another family at another time through a mutual friend who noted the similarities in our lifestyle. Perhaps God would use a home schooler's meeting or something similar to arrange the circumstances. God's Spirit knows how to meet this need for our lives.

One word of advice that I can give from our experience is this: do not fall for misplaced guilt that teachings on the "assembling of yourselves together" (Hebrews 10:25) sometimes cause. Those who want to promote their organization will often use this Scripture to try to make us feel we are forsaking the assembling of ourselves if we are not "committed" to a local church group, on a membership roster, or at least committed to regular attendance as the leadership requires.

Do not fall victim to this false guilt; God knows just the right amount and the right timing for our assembling with other Christians for the exhorting of one another. We have found that if we are diligent in the Spirit to have frequent times throughout the week of Bible discussion and relating all of life to the Scriptures together as a family, that the need for assembling together with others is not as frequent as some would have us to think. Christian assembling can be done out of rote duty like most everything else, and it is best to feel Spirit led in this.

Actually when we read this verse on the assembling together in Hebrews 10 in context, we find it is addressing those who were trying to avoid assembling together because they knew the teaching would bring conviction upon certain behavior in their life. They were wanting to sin intentionally—"...for if we sin willfully..." (Hebrews 10:26.) Those that were forsaking the assembly were doing so because they willfully wanted to sin, and they didn't want to be convicted for it by the preaching or teaching they might hear. However, our experience among home schooling families is that many of them have a higher standard of righteousness for their family than what is usually being presented and what is being exemplified by the social interaction within these churches. They are not forsaking because they want to sin, but generally because they do *not* want to sin, or they do not want their children to face certain temptations.

We know many home schooling families who, like ourselves, have even avoided church attendance altogether from time to time and have just stayed home and worshipped as a family rather than subject their families to wrong teaching and examples. I think this sometimes just must be done for Christ's sake; but God is faithful, and He will in His timing bring along the proper opportunities for our families to meet for exhortation with other Christians.

Neither do we have to have three songs, a prayer, the passing of the offering plate, and a sermon to be functioning properly as a Christian assembly. I think some order is helpful and important with an orderly, worshipful room and format, but there should be flexibility. Take turns among the qualified men in bringing a topical message or at other times work through a book of the Bible. It is good to allow for the men (both young and old) to have opportunity for sharing a Biblical insight or personal testimony which would provide for the "edifying of one another". We do observe the need for the function of a "ruling" elder in the group where a father, who seems to more closely display the qualities described in I Timothy 3 and Titus, should perhaps be more respected for their viewpoint, although

we should all be able to minister to some degree to each other—"...as every man has received the gift, even so minister the same one to another, as good stewards of the manifold grace of God." (I Peter 4:10.)

We do not feel there is a need to collect an offering. The bulk of the expense in most churches is the building fund and paying the pastor and other personnel, and, of course, with the home church or smaller assembly these expenses can be avoided. Giving can be directed to meet more important needs among Christian brethren like supporting poor Christians and missionary works, etc. Perhaps collecting a fund for meeting special needs of those within your church group may be helpful from time to time. Much of the giving described in the N.T. seems to be directed at meeting the needs of the poorer Christians; this seems to be a blessed way to give.

Neither does a church have to have a certain, substantial number present or to always be emphasizing the view that we are trying to "build up" the size of our church. The Lord is still "adding" to the church in His omniscient way. I do not feel it is wise to be trying to work at building an organization. We need to be faithful in ministering to one another, and God will add in His omniscient way and timing!

Today many Christians are of the opinion that big is always better, and this is far from the truth. I have talked with brothers who are involved in home churches and smaller assemblies who feel that groups should be purposely limited in size to allow for a more intimate interaction between brothers and sisters. Today we are hearing of more and more large assemblies that are organizing smaller, mid-week, cell group ministries at various homes. These large churches are realizing their inability to minister to specific needs in their large assemblies. Even though many are afraid to dismantle their organization, their very practice of having "cell group" meetings testifies that they recognize some inadequacies in their larger group meetings.

God is faithful; watch for the opportunities He brings along. He will meet our needs to assemble together in a way that will

not be detrimental to the Godliness we desire in our homes. But what if it doesn't seem like God is bringing another family along at present? What should we do? It has been my observation that when a Christian man begins to display in his life the qualifications for leadership, and when our children are at a maturity level where they are not as vulnerable, God will bring along others for this man and his family to minister to in some way. Most of the qualifications for leadership (discussed in a later chapter) in I Timothy 3 and Titus revolve around a man's ability to be a spiritual leader at home.

He has an exemplary marriage; he has spent time daily in the Word meditating on Scripture and applying it to situations in his own life and home; and he has children who are faithful (which means they are not only believing, but living a life of faith), children who are not unruly in any way and that have a purity and integrity of morals ("...not accused of riot or unruly" –Titus 1:6). One cannot expect his family to become this way overnight. He will need to spend a *lot* of concentrated time on his own home for a season. God may purposely keep our involvement with other families to a minimum until He sees us approaching these kinds of qualities at home first; then He will bring others along.

If God doesn't seem to be bringing along another family with whom you feel comfortable, then maybe it is still best for your home to remain a little more separate for a while so that your home can be more thoroughly established, strengthened, and settled before ministry begins. God may keep your involvements with other Christians a little irregular, or you may even feel a little isolated at times. Use these times to build closeness and unity and to find fulfillment within your own marriage and family. God will expand your ministry and your involvement with others when you are best prepared.

Throughout this time of waiting, take advantage of opportunities for personal evangelism and look for other ways to minister as a family. Not all of us are called to specifically have church ministries. We can sometimes operate a ministry in a similar capacity as a church ministry by serving the Lord in

other ways. For example, I know of some home schooling families who have ministries in nursing homes. I know of some who have singing ministries where they have opportunity to teach and preach the Word. Some families have fairly regular opportunities to minister to other families by inviting another family over for dinner followed with a time of hymn singing and Bible discussion. We know of home schooling families who have weekly Bible studies with other like-minded families, with hopes that in time these meetings will evolve into church assemblies.

We do feel that as God begins to give opportunities to minister that it is best to keep things on a spiritual plane, meeting together for edification, encouragement, preaching, exhorting, and worship on a spiritual level centered around Godliness and purity. Too much involvement on a social level only tends to distract from this function of assembling together. "Not forsaking the assembling but *exhorting* one another." Exhorting is the primary purpose for meeting together. A meal together every so often seems to enhance the unity of believers, but when this becomes too frequent or when other social activity like games or sports begin to get involved, then we tend to drift into socializing. The big evangelical churches in America today have been called social clubs for years; we don't want to fall into this same pattern on a smaller scale.

- Handling Disruptive Families -

What should be done if after meeting with another family for a while, we begin to discover some major differences or concerns that are creating problems for our home? We would urge families not to "jump" into a church arrangement with another family; take enough time to be sure you feel pretty comfortable with each other's convictions and lifestyle. But if you do find yourself in a home church situation where perhaps your children are being negatively influenced by the children of another family, or there arises some other major concern, and the offending family doesn't seem to want to change or they change a little but are still presenting negatives you are troubled with,

it may be time to reconsider whether or not you should continue meeting together.

Another problem possibility is a new family beginning to attend your home group meeting who is presenting negtatives. I don't believe there is anything wrong with church attendance being on the "invitation" basis for a while with some potentially disruptive families. Paul mentions letters of commendation in regards to some Christians; there is sometimes a need to be a little selective until a core nucleus of families is established with whom you feel comfortable. If a family then begins to attend who is disruptive and they do not seem to be adapting to the example of the "core families" with child training (or some other similar problem), then maybe the men in the group might want to have a discussion with the father of this family over some of the concerns. In every church meeting, there will be the need for such men's meetings to address concerns that may arise within the church. Trying to handle these problems tactfully with love and prayer is important in minimizing hurt feelings.

Sometimes we can discern or sense that a family is presenting problems out of ignorance, and this family may need time to change. With other families, you may discern improper motives and sense they do not want to genuinely change in heart; after giving them sufficient time and encouragement to change, you may find it would be best not to continue fellowshipping with them. Sometimes we have a ministry in some people's lives for a while, and then it's time to go on, or maybe God would want us to divide so that He can expand our sphere of influence. We have found with our children now being older, we can tolerate some problems with people who need help with family life and child training, but there was a time when ours were younger when we were cautious about exposing them to wrong influences, other children, and adults alike.

- Preparing for Ministry -

It seems for some that the time of preparation for ministry is the hardest to complete. We can be so easily tempted that we

are not serving the Lord, or that we are too "home" oriented. Don't allow these temptations to get you to start "working in the energy of the flesh" to serve the Lord. The home needs to be thoroughly established before getting too involved in other ministry, or your family may suffer for it.

Husbands and wives together must discern just the right "burden" of ministry for their own family to successfully bear at any given point of their life. Jesus said His yoke was easy and burden was light. When we are yoked with the Lord doing the work He has for us, there will be some burden, but there will be little stress. But when we are pushing ourselves and begin working in the flesh, then someone in the family will be over burdened, and a degree of stress or strain will be noticed. Give heed to these warning signs and be willing to prune back some of your involvements if you are sensing some of this strain.

During this time of waiting and preparation, spend your time on meditation in Scripture and applying it to daily life. Some men may feel the need for more formal Bible training before attempting to lead a group. There are a number of correspondence Bible school programs available to fathers and older sons who feel this need, although much of what is taught in Bible schools can be learned through reading and personal study (the same books used in Bible schools are available to anyone). This kind of home–based Bible training is preferable because it doesn't disrupt the home; fathers and sons can still keep their occupations, and the real classroom of everyday life is not disrupted. I believe that as the home church movement grows, there will be more of this self help training available to fathers and older sons, similar to what we find with the curriculum suppliers for home schooling mothers.

However, I don't want it to sound like an intellectual grasp of truth is our goal either. James 1:20 says there is something very deceiving about mere intellectual knowledge of God's Word. Our real goal in teaching and leadership is to speak from experience, to share how Scripture has been lived out as a part of daily life. Christendom today is filled with babes in Christ who are preoccupied and crammed with intellectual knowledge of

the Word of God. They certainly "ought to be teachers" (Hebrews 5:12), but they still need to be taught because they haven't learned to live out Scripture and then to communicate this experience with others. By simplifying our intake of truth and allowing God to form this truth in our life through grace, we can begin to build this experiential knowledge.

Chapter Four

What About Doctrinal Differences?

For years we have been setting the basis for our fellowship with other Christians mostly on theological or doctrinal views, and there is certainly a value in being "sound" in doctrine. But many Christians are coming to realize that a real and perhaps more important criteria for evaluating how "sound" someone is in doctrine lies in their lifestyle, not just their denominational or theological views or background. In other words, if someone really has a good grasp of God's truth, it will be evidenced in their manner of life; you will see Godly "fruit" in their lives and homes.

For centuries, Christians have been drawing up battle lines over theological views or interpretation of certain passages of Scriptures, and regardless of one's Godliness, as long as they agree on interpretation, they can be friends; but if they don't agree, then someone is accused of being "off" or not walking with the Lord. Of course, denominations and Christian sects have been excluding one another for years for these reasons.

When we as a family consider fellowshipping with other Christian families, we usually give some consideration to their theological background because we know some denominational or sectarian groups have drifted farther from true holiness and

into more worldliness than others. Thus we know somewhat what to expect as far as the purity of conduct and worldly involvement of families or individuals based upon their denominational or sectarian affiliations. But generally the most important consideration should be this family's or individual's desire for Godly living, not whether they are labeled with a particular denominational name.

I think it's time for Christians in America to stop excluding one another over such differences and other more minor theological points. Let us begin, as much as possible, "receiving one another" and working towards the goal of becoming "like-minded" in areas of interpretation or theology. Our central objective should be to seek those and ask God to bring to us those who have this primary goal of a Godly home in mind. If we are clear on this objective, a good degree of like-mindness is already present.

We have observed that among home schooling families this is generally often the reason they have chosen to home school; they are attempting to keep their children from secular type influences, and they want a Godly home. But unfortunately this is not always the case. To some, home schooling is a preference rather than a conviction; to others, intellectual superiority is their objective rather than building Godly character in their children. Therefore just because someone home schools doesn't guarantee that they are a good candidate for fellowship.

Still other home schooling parents have left their children undisciplined and have few Godly objectives in mind for their homes. Others have been convinced that a leader must be seminary trained or that their church group must be one of the major denominations, and sometimes we find that theological views are so diverse between families that the potential for harmonizing such views would be impossible or at least very difficult.

Among home schoolers there is a wide spectrum of different theological-doctrinal backgrounds, and we have found that sometimes these differences can be overlooked or tolerated to

some degree. But what do we do about legitimate differences in these areas? These differences in theology can certainly cause divisions even among those of us who have this one central goal in mind of building the Godly home. Inevitably, our adversary will attempt to bring up these differences, even minor differences, in an effort to drive a wedge between believers or to cause division and strife.

We have faced this when assembling with others in our home, and I believe the consensus has been to try to keep these doctrinal differences in the background and to rather focus on the vast majority of Scripture in which we do agree. Besides, it is seldom that two Christians agree absolutely on every interpretation of every passage of Scripture anyway, so why allow these differences to cause division? Later on, once a unity and like-mindedness has grown with another family, perhaps then you may want to bring up a discussion on some of these controversial matters of doctrine or theology or interpretation. But be prepared to agree to disagree, and let it be at that. Maintain a spirit of love and allow God to bring about a spirit of like-mindedness in His timing on such areas of difference. Romans 14 seems to be giving some guidelines for these controversial issues. "Accept him who is weak in the faith without passing judgment on disputable matters." (Romans 14:1.)

Don't fall into either judging or despising one another as described in vs. 3 in this chapter but seek after the peace and unity described in vs. 19. "Let us therefore follow after the things which make for peace, and things wherewith one may edify another."

Now when it comes to moral issues, Romans 14:21 and other passages warn against the danger of putting stumbling blocks in our brothers' path; so on issues like holy and pure greetings, modest apparel among the women and men, proper music for the meetings, and purity of speech in the preaching and discussions, etc., there should be no compromise on these issues. Of course, there will still be the need for patience and love; we are all on different levels of growth in holy living and Biblical wisdom, and new converts and those coming from worldly

churches will need some time to make changes in these areas. But in areas of disputable theology or doctrine, I think we should accept one another and not allow these differences to cause division if this is at all possible. It is not always easy to receive one another and allow God in His time to cause a blending process to take place along theological or interpretational views, but this is the best path that leads to "peace and wherewith we may edify one another." Paul believed Christians with different convictions could live together in harmony, and we have seen this happen in our own group.

-What About Setting Rules and Regulations?-

We don't feel it is a good idea to try to make a set of rules in an attempt to symbolize or legislate holiness within your group. By this I mean setting up creeds or codes of conduct such as: attendance expectations, membership requirements, tithing requirements, uniformity of dress codes, required ordinance observations, absolute theological likeness or other requirements or rules that tend to override God's free working of grace and discernment in the hearts and lives of the individual Christian. Such regulations often contribute to a decline in discernment of right and wrong, and in the promptings and leadings of the Spirit. We do as a church group want to shun the liberal lifestyle and philosophies of the world around us while at the same time remaining free from lapsing into following certain rules, codes, or other so-called Biblically based legalisms that often diminish the free exercise of discernment and wisdom.

We do want to accept the individual Biblical convictions that individuals may have acquired either through the personal study of God's Word or through traditional church upbringing. By this I mean convictions in such areas as baptisms, partaking of the Lord's Supper, head coverings (wearing or not wearing a physical head covering), and other similar convictions, striving for a like-mindedness as much as possible and avoiding the debating and strife that sometimes arises due to differing convictions and interpretations. We would urge groups to follow the spirit of Romans 14:19. "Let us therefore follow after the

things which make for peace and things wherewith one may edify another." Far too often today groups that require adherence to certain ordinances, codes, or beliefs fall into comparing and judging and far too often excluding others from their circle of fellowship over these issues; and sadly many times they are relatively minor issues. The early church did not attempt to legislate such things but rather relied on the Godly example of leadership and sound teaching to promote this within the church.

> *"Yet unlike some later religious groups, the early Christians generally didn't try to legislate righteousness; instead they relied on sound teaching and righteous example. Religious groups that depended on extensive rules to produce personal holiness usually ended up producing Pharisees instead. For this reason, the church emphasized the need for new believers to change from the inside out. Externals were considered worthless unless they reflected what was happening inside a person."*

(From *Will The Real Heretics Please Stand Up,* Scroll Publishing Co., pp. 50 , 51.)

The Apostle Paul struggled with the churches at Colosse and Galatia over these issues. They were desiring to return to a legal system and asceticism as a means to obtaining or symbolizing righteousness. Paul also warned of the ineffectiveness of turning back from the power of grace to such legal systems in other major sections of his writings. Paul does urge the Christian to be constantly discerning the expediency of every practice in the Christian life either individually or corporately. "All things are lawful, but all things are not expedient; all things are lawful for me, but all things edify not." (I Cor. 10:23.) He is constantly encouraging the Christian to evaluate what they are doing and to consider if it is going to lead to Godly edification or building up of holy living. This was really the purpose for assembling together. Grace is the power that brings this holiness about.

- General Guidelines -

It would be helpful to set some general guidelines, however, with our main purpose and goal being that of holiness. With this in mind each attendee should be encouraged to regularly appraise their apparel for modesty and purity. We realize that tastes in modest apparel often change as time goes by, and we become more holy and discerning in our Christian walk; so there needs to be a sense of tolerance that allows for this maturity of discernment.

Orderliness also requires that children should be managed and maintained in orderly demeanor as much as possible by parents. Here again, tolerance and patience will be essential as parents grow in discernment on how to achieve this. We would encourage families to sit together during services, and younger children to stay with parents under their supervision during meals or fellowship time. Pre-teen and teens who are proper in conduct can be allowed to range more freely. Generally, infants can be a part of the worship service, but when crying or fussing becomes too interruptive, it might be best for the child to be taken away from the meeting area for a while.

During sharing time of the service where musical presentations, testimonials, prayer requests, or any other type of public announcements are given, they should be proper and in keeping with a holy church setting. Proper music types are not easily learned and may require the help of the more mature Christian's discernment. All public speaking should be clear of moral description that may be embarrassing, awkward, or the least offensive. Again, in general, wives and daughters are limited in their speaking in the church assembly, and their thoughts and insights can be expressed appropriately to the congregation by their husbands or fathers. Some announcements or comments from wives or daughters may be appropriate at times, with discretion. Wives and daughters can bring musical presentations with brief announcements provided they have been approved by their own husbands or fathers.

We do want to set a Godly example for those who come to our meetings. We want to exemplify modest apparel; pure and

holy greetings; parents responsibly keeping their children in order (some parents may need teachings on how to begin this); an orderly and worshipful atmosphere; proper Godly music; pure speech which would include avoiding references to T.V., movies and other secular forms of idolatry or entertainment, or other ungodly practices in the world around us; and holy and pure conduct with those of all ages. Therefore, a few generalized rules of conduct such as these lightly enforced may be necessary to help keep orderliness in the setting.

But when groups begin to set down certain codes or creeds that are supposed to uniquely set us aside from others which, in a sense, can give us our own righteousness after our own "laws", we tend to fail to evaluate our hearts from a conscience point of view; and inevitably, there will be those who get around the cracks found in our laws. As long as we are following the rules set up by the leaders in our groups, we "think" we are doing pretty well within our own group. But eventually and inevitably what begins to happen is we compare our rules and corresponding conduct with the rules set up by other groups, and walls and barriers of defense go up. We begin to have a righteousness of our own in keeping with our own group's rules, regulations, or interpretation. And, of course, the other groups are considered "off" (even though they may have some very good holy ways in many respects of their own) just because they are not following the rules of our own group, whether they be written or just understood. By "comparing ourselves among ourselves" in such ways, we are actually demonstrating a lack of wisdom and maturity in our Christian life.

"And be found in Him, not having mine own righteousness which is of the Law, but that which is through the faith of Christ, the righteousness which is of God by faith..." (Quote of the Apostle Paul from Phil. 3:9.) Furthermore Paul warned the Galatian church, which had begun to set standards of righteousness in keeping with the Judaic law, that if they even attempted to set up and keep the least of those laws (thinking that this would make them righteous) they would begin to "fall away from grace." (See Galatians 5:4.)

I am definitely not saying that we shouldn't have some standards or goals of righteousness; we very much should. We should be constantly evaluating the purity, holiness, and Godliness in our own lives individually and within our church group as a whole, but we simply should not try to set a certain list of rules that legislate this. Actually the "edifying of itself in love" coupled with the power of grace and the Godly example from the leadership was the way the early church moved more and more towards holy living. Christian brothers and sisters exhorted each other in holy ways and confessed their faults one to another; and when they recognized how certain of their practices had led to a hindrance in the progress of holy living and to other deficiencies, they began to make changes and prayed for one another. This is a better and more Biblical way of reaching greater heights of righteousness within our groups, rather than setting up a list of rules or a church creed to achieve this.

Consider how the early church established standards of righteousness for their assemblies; this was accomplished mostly by the example set by those in leadership. The younger or less mature and experienced Christians were to "submit themselves to the elder." They were to copy the example of those who were in leadership. This required above all that those in leadership not only have an understanding from Scripture of basic, proper, righteous, holy ways, but that they also exemplified it by their lifestyle.

Through this approach the churches soon became islands of purity, exemplifying a Godly culture within the ungodly culture of the world. Those who came to their churches were able to shake off the sins of the world by conforming to this new culture found within the churches.

The Godly standard of a church must begin at the top with the leadership. In the following chapters I discuss the qualifications for setting or ordaining leadership in the Christian assembly. Whether we plan to have an assembly in our own home or whether we hope to sit under others in an assembly somewhere else, a careful evaluation of those in leadership based on

these qualifications will give us further wisdom in being able to discern the impact such an assembly will have on our homes.

Chapter Five

Leadership Objectives

For years in America, we have been evaluating church leaders on an incomplete and inadequate basis for judging soundness. In general, leaders are selected on the basis of two or three general criteria. Usually we first look at what Bible school or institution they attended, and their corresponding academic performance there. Then in addition to this evaluation of the candidate's head knowledge of Scripture or doctrine, we consider such things as personal charisma, charm, or personality. Finally we allow this candidate to demonstrate his speaking abilities.

Although Paul's directives for selecting leadership do emphasize giving sufficient consideration to a brother's soundness in doctrine and his corresponding ability to communicate this effectively with those that hear him, these points alone are only a very small part in making a total evaluation of a brother's "desire for the office of a bishop or leader." (I Tim. 3:16.)

It is also apparent that Paul did not assume or propose that such a man's leadership abilities were to be acquired at a

school. Spiritual growth, soundness in doctrine, communication skills, and Godly character were to be a product of the ministry of the church over a long period of time where a man's Christian character and discernment could be consistently demonstrated to those in attendance. Paul states in Titus, Chapter Two, that young men in the church were to show a pattern of good works in such areas as soundness of doctrine, and seriousness and sincerity of faith; the church was the place where Godly leadership qualities were to be learned and passed on. Early church leadership was perpetuated and transferred to others through this system.

In fact, as we consider Paul's directives for selecting leadership in local churches as stated in two of his final letters (Timothy and Titus), we find that the description of a man's ability to lead encompasses his total lifestyle and how this is manifested to those closest to him. Such things to be considered were: his personal faith and consistency of walk with Christ; the quality of his marriage and his wife's walk with Christ; the conduct, faith, and consistency of the Godly character of his children; his practical Bible knowledge and his ability to sanctify and teach with it; his ability to oversee such areas as his own home life, his self control, his lack of personal greed, his reputation towards those in secular circles, and so on. So we see that when judging one's soundness, we must look far deeper than intellectual abilities or speaking abilities. One's true Christian character, lifestyle, and results of his Christian experience will be the best basis for judging "soundness".

Christians, for the first few centuries, followed these directives, but today we have drifted from these guidelines. Those who have studied extensively early church history have observed that early church fathers for the first couple centuries after the New Testament period followed closely to Paul's directives:

"The church-wide commitment of the early Christians was a direct reflection of the quality of their leadership.
Today's evangelical churches are typically governed by

a pastor and a body of elders and/or a board of deacons. Normally, the pastor is a professionally-trained man with a seminary degree who wasn't raised in the congregation that has hired him. Frequently, he has no governing authority in the congregation other than the power of persuasion. The body of elders or board of deacons are normally men with full-time secular jobs. They oversee church finances and programs, and they often establish church policy. But typically, no one in the church goes to them for spiritual counseling, and they aren't usually the shepherds of the flock.

Although we use many of the same names for church leaders as did the early Christians—such as "elders" and "deacons"—our church government differs considerably from theirs in *substance*. Instead of a sole professional pastor, the entire body of elders were the full-time pastors in the early churches. *The oldest or most gifted elder was usually appointed as the chairman of the body of elders.* He was generally called the overseer (bishop) or superintendent of the congregation. The overseer and elders weren't outsiders brought into the congregation; they had generally lived in it for years. Their strengths and weaknesses were well known to the entire congregation.

Furthermore, they didn't qualify to serve as overseers or elders by studying in school and stuffing their heads with knowledge. The congregation wasn't as interested in the depth of their knowledge as they were in the depth of their *spirituality*. How close was the man to God? Had he lived for years as an example to other Christians? Was he ready to lay down his life for Christ? As Tertullian told the Romans, 'Our elders are proven men who obtain their position not by purchase, but by established character.'

There were no seminaries. A man learned the necessary skills to be an elder through the school of experience. He was trained by the existing body of elders, and he learned how to walk closely with God and to shepherd others by seeing and imitating their example. He was given hands-on

experience under their supervision and was allowed to make mistakes. He had to be able to teach by example as well as by word before he could even be considered for service as an elder or overseer". (From *Will The Real Heretics Please Stand Up,* Scroll Publishing Co., pp. 52, 53.)

Today we are hearing more and more teachings that are attempting to convince Christians that we should separate the character of our leaders from their position of leadership. We are hearing those who assert that church leaders and pastors should be allowed to have just as many struggles with their personal Christian lives, their marriages, and children as anyone else in the church. Of course, the reason we are observing this false persuasion is because many Christian lay people (especially home schooling parents) are beginning to see through the facade of intellectualism and mere talk, and they are beginning to once again evaluate the true Christian character of those in leadership.

The whole issue of character in leadership is obscured today, and our adversary has a very important reason for keeping it obscure; he knows the leadership position is, above all, an exampleship position. Our adversary knows that we learn far more from an example than we do from words of instruction. We tend to copy the example of other lives. And, of course, if a man is a proper example to others, his words and teachings will be correspondingly accurate because he will be able to speak from proven experience. So Paul states that we are to be "sound in doctrine as leaders", but above all we are to have a good track record of proven, successful, Christian experience and character as evidenced in lifestyle and home life.

- Paul's Directives for a Plural Ministry -

When one studies the subject of church leadership from the Scriptures, we come away also with overwhelming evidence that every church had a plurality of leadership. We do not find any instances where one man ran a particular church for any

indefinite length of time alone.

Every church had elders, plural. Now granted, it appears that one or two of these elders seems to have been a pastor (such as James); but he probably would be more accurately described as the senior, presiding, or ruling elder (or superintendent); at least he or none other in the N.T. was addressed as pastor. "It (the New Testament) nowhere raises one presbyter (leader or bishop) above the rest, and clothes him with a special dignity as (the) bishop." (*History of the Christian Church,* Hendrickson Publishers, Vol. 1, p. 124.) Because of his experience, age, and wisdom, perhaps his spiritual opinion may have carried more weight than that of the other elders. Decisions and opinions seemed to have been arrived at corporately by the leaders, as in Acts, Chapter Fifteen, with one elder (James) summarizing the consensus of opinion of the leaders.

When considering the prospects of a home church or a similar smaller assembly, some might be puzzled as to how such a small group could afford to hire a single pastor. Well, the early churches did not have a concern in this area because the apostles' tradition was to ordain or appoint elders (plural) from the laity in every church to be the ministers. There was no distinct entity called the clergy in the early church. We personally have discovered that by sharing in the leadership and preaching or teaching responsibilities with several men, this allows for more time for each leader to "prepare" before having to speak again. Messages seem to be more of an expression of the burden of the heart, in keeping with one's own spiritual gift, targeting specific needs or concerns rather than something just prepared as a matter of routine. We have often remarked at how the Spirit of the Lord brought along just the perfect message to meet our needs at the perfect time through this preaching arrangement.

Another important aspect to this cooperative ministry which we have observed is that it allows for children to see their own fathers being a part of the leadership, or preparing for it in the church. This tends to enhance the loyalty of wives and children to their own husbands and fathers, which in turn strengthens

the structure of the individual homes. Children are motivated to follow in the footsteps of their own fathers. Sons can begin in the teen years preparing for a future of ministry that can be passed on to them from their own fathers or other elders in the group. In any group where there is this spirit of mutual edification, everyone (young and old) becomes much more motivated to serve the Lord with their life. Furthermore, with this shared ministry arrangement, it becomes unnecessary to have to arrange to pay some man to do this, and giving can be directed to meet other needs such as supporting poorer Christians or missionary concerns.

It is true that the Scriptures indicate that some financial compensation was to be given to some elders ministering to the group, particularly if the burden of teaching and ministry has occupied so much of his time that he (one who *labored* in the Word) was unable to work to support his needs or those of his family. But, Paul makes it clear that for himself, he did not seek or desire such compensation; in fact, he states that his own employment (tent making) had not only supplied his own needs but also the needs of those that were with him. (Acts 20:34.) Later when Paul was in prison and could not work, he accepted support from churches. It is possible that some elders, perhaps an older man in ministry, may find the burdens and expansion of the ministry to require some support from the other brothers from time to time, but, in general, churches with a plural ministry will find it unneedful to have to make plans for supporting a single leader.

There are numerous references to the plural ministry in the New Testament. For example, Paul states in his letter to the church in Rome that he was confident that *they* were able to admonish one another; evidently there was more than one involved in the ministry there.

I have already mentioned how the church in Jerusalem which was quite large had at least nineteen men in leadership. A second church we find mentioned in the book of Acts is the church at Antioch. "Now they which were scattered abroad upon the persecution that arose about Stephen travelled as far

as Phenice, and Cyprus, and Antioch, preaching the Word to none but unto the Jews only. Some of them, however, men from Cyprus and Cyrene went to Antioch and began to speak to Greeks also, telling them the good news about the Lord Jesus. The Lord's hand was with them, and a great number of people believed and turned to the Lord. News of this reached the ears of the church at Jerusalem, and they sent Barnabus to Antioch." (Acts 11:19-22.)

Then Barnabus went and found Paul and brought him to Antioch; and the two of them ministered to the group, and the group began to grow. So we see that this church started with some evangelists from Cyprus and Cyrene; then Barnabus, a prophet or teacher, was sent to them for a while. Then came Paul, the apostle, to join in with the ministry.

This church may have begun with one leader, but it did not long remain so. Barnabus was first sent out from the church at Jerusalem to join in the ministry in Antioch; he apparently felt the need for more help. At least he did not try to do it all alone. He called Paul to help him with this work. In time, the church had grown, and in Acts 13:1 we find that there were now no less than five men ministering to the group at Antioch—Barnabus, Niger, Lucius, Manaen, and Paul. "Now there were in the church that was at Antioch certain prophets and teachers; as Barnabus, and Simeon that was called Niger, and Lucius of Cyrene and Manaen, which had been brought up with Herod the Tetrarch, and Saul (Paul)." So we see this church had many in leadership with a diversity of gifts.

Paul, in retracing his steps on his first missionary tour (Acts 14:22, 23), ordained elders (plural) in every church. The word elder could also be translated as pastor, overseer, or bishop. Later we find that Paul left Titus at Crete (Titus 1:5) to set things in order. Titus was told to ordain elders (plural) in every city. We have no record that more than one church existed in these cities. It is also implied that elders were chosen from the local group and not normally brought in from outside places.

Of the many references that speak of the ministry in a definite church organization, it is referred to most often in the

plural. Concerning the church at Ephesus, Acts 20:17 reads: "And from Miletus, he (Paul) sent to Ephesus and called the elders of the church." Note that it does not say Paul called the elders of the churches (plural). There was one church with several elders in leadership.

At Philippi, Paul addresses the bishops or elders and the deacons (plural) without making reference to a single pastor or leader. "Paul and Timotheus, the servants of Jesus Christ, to all the saints in Christ Jesus which are at Philippi, with the bishops and deacons".

In addressing the church at Thessalonica, Paul urges the brethren to "know them (plural) which are over you in the Lord and admonish (teach) you." Note the plural teaching ministry. In Crete, Paul directs Titus to "ordain elders" (plural) in every church. Paul directs Timothy to do the same for the individual churches in Asia Minor.

In other general references to the individual churches (such as Hebrews 13:7— "Remember them (plural) which have the rule over you"; I Peter 5:1— "The elders (plural) which are among you, I exhort who am also an elder"; and James 5:14— "Is any sick among you, let him call for the elders (plural) of the church"—the leadership is not singular but plural in all these instances. The apostolic tradition was to set a plural ministry in churches.

Some will assert that Timothy and Titus were actual pastors in respective churches, and it is possible that they assumed a role of singular pastors in these churches for a time to "set things in order". Timothy and Titus were more accurately Paul's emissaries for establishing sound teaching in various churches, just as Barnabus was for a while with the church in Antioch; but they were obviously not to remain permanently in this position. The elders were to assume this role of leadership: "Set things in order and ordain (other) elders in every city".

It is logical for a newly formed church to require the teaching and ministry of a more mature Christian leader to establish the new church in principle and policy. But eventually, Paul wanted each of these churches to be able to "minister to itself" with a

plural ministry chosen from among their members. So it may be plausible that a newly formed house church may require some ministry from the elders of a sister church, or perhaps just have one leader for a while until elders or leaders can be designated for this new church. Particularly if the house church is comprised of new or recent converts, spiritual growth is certainly required for one to take a position of leadership. The early churches had several men in leadership with perhaps one of these men being senior or ruling elder with other younger men aspiring to and preparing for future leadership roles.

It is also possible that perhaps in a small assembly there may be no one who actually feels "qualified" to assume a role of leadership. When Paul sent Timothy and Titus to ordain elders in their respective assemblies, those Christians had already been meeting together for some time. Perhaps there were several men or families already working together, encouraging one another to be reaching forth towards these Godly qualifications. I think it is very probable and understandable that some beginning house churches or other assemblies may see the need for the men to concentrate above all on their individual families, seeking these qualities at home first, which will prepare them for the role of leadership in the church.

Years ago when we first started meeting with one or two other families in our own home, our discussions seemed to be constantly revolving around the marriage, child training, and other home oriented thoughts and Scripture. I don't believe we realized that what we were actually doing was encouraging one another in the qualities that would eventually in part lead us to becoming qualified church leaders. I have observed that many home schooling families are simply alone today, having church as a family, particularly those families with younger children. When our children were younger (early teen years and younger), my wife and I felt they were more vulnerable to influence, so we were very selective with our fellowship. We used this less active social period in our life to build the unity and strength of our marriage and Godly character in our children while working towards the goal of meeting the qualifications for leader-

ship outlined in Paul's letters to Timothy and Titus.

In the following chapter, I would like to look a little deeper into these qualifications for leadership set forth by Paul to Timothy and Titus. However, before going into this discussion, I would first like to say this. I don't believe these qualifications are necessarily set up as a basis to disqualify a man from leadership. They are probably designed to be a description of the Godly *objectives* every Christian man should be reaching for in his own life. We are all on various levels of maturity in our Christian experience, and God intends for us to minister our proven Christian experience and knowledge, along with our particular spiritual gifts, with others in some capacity of Christian service or ministry. Neither does a man have to completely manifest these qualifications before he can minister his own particular spiritual gift or insight for the edifying of the brethren in some way. However in the church assembly, he may be more limited in his position as an example to the flock, and also in his capacity to take the authority in the group on certain matters or spiritual concerns.

- What About Being "Called To Preach"? -

In my years of Christian experience, I have encountered from time to time those who hold that being "called to preach" is pretty well all that is needed in being a leader. I believe that being called to preach may be similar to having the desire to be a bishop - "If a man desires the office of a bishop (leader), he desires a good work." (I Tim. 3:1.) But there is a big difference between having a desire or call to preach from God and having the qualifications to lead (qualifications are described in the next chapter). I believe many men experience this God-ordained burden to preach or teach, but God also wants to prepare and qualify those so called for the task ahead. Moses sensed a "call" to lead out the Children of Israel when he was 40 years of age when he slew the Egyptian. But it wasn't until 40 years later that he became, through life's experience, qualified in character to lead them. When God calls us, we must also allow God through His training to qualify us for this ministry.

Chapter Six
Spiritual Gifts and Leadership Qualifications

For years now the emphasis in the church has been on individual spiritual gifts (not that spiritual gifts are unimportant), but there has been little regard given to a man having the qualifications to minister such gifts. Paul addresses both issues in his letters.

In Paul's earlier letters, such as I Corinthians (written A.D. 55-57), the subject of spiritual gifts is very prominent, and we find little mention of qualifications for leadership. With the progress of time, we see in Paul's subsequent letters such as Ephesians, Colossians, and Philippians less emphasis on spiritual gifts and greater emphasis on qualifications for ministering gifts as individual believers. For example, Ephesians and Colossians were probably written four or five years after I Corinthians, and in these letters discussion of spiritual gifts is more summarized; and we see Paul beginning to emphasize teachings addressed more to character and conduct in the Christian home. Ephesians and Colossians both address the issues of marriage and child training, whereas his earlier letters are less instructive in these areas.

Finally, in Paul's last letters, I and II Timothy and Titus,

written three to five years after Ephesians and Colossians, we see very little mentioned in the area of gifts, and rather a great deal of teaching on the subject of qualifications for leadership. The central theme of these qualifications revolves around the leader's marriage and his ability to guide and minister in his own home first. "For if a man know not how to rule his own house, how shall he take care of the church of God?" (I Tim. 3:5.) So we see somewhat of a transition in Paul's thought pattern in these areas over a ten year period.

In the Apostle Peter's letters, which were probably written about the same time as Paul's last letters of Timothy and Titus, we see a discussion of spiritual gifts, Christian marriage qualities, and emphasis that leaders were to be proper examples to the flock altogether. I believe it would be fair to conclude that Paul, the chiefest apostle, like Peter would have considered a man's spiritual gift as very important, but his qualifications for ministering this gift within the church to be just as important.

For years in Christian circles, we have erroneously looked primarily at a man's gift or his intellectual head knowledge of Scripture in designating him for a position of ministry; Paul urges us to look much deeper. It is not uncommon for Christians today to look around and see one who is a gifted evangelist or teacher or perhaps a young man who has the gift of shepherding (pastoring), give them a few years of Bible school, and then elevate them to a singular position of church leadership. In such churches where the emphasis is primarily on spiritual gifts such as the Corinthian church, we generally see a church that encounters many temptations and problems. But, when we take the combination of spiritual gifts, a plural ministry, and setting men over the congregation who have met the proper qualifications for leadership, we have the best combination for a successful church ministry.

I have seen evangelists alone heading churches, men who never first reached the qualifications for leadership as described in I Timothy and Titus. Consequently what happened in their churches was that this evangelist emphasized evangelism so much, with a disregard for the home and related spiritual

growth, that many of their followers began to disregard the spiritual needs of their homes, and they spent all their time focusing on evangelism. Unfortunately they evangelized a few in the world, but lost a few from their own families. However, if we put an evangelist in the place of plural eldership in our church after having demonstrated the qualifications for leadership as described in I Timothy 3 and Titus, we would have an evangelist who thoroughly understood putting his home first, and consequently he would not over emphasize evangelism at the expense of the home.

Furthermore, evangelists tend to have less depth of spiritual knowledge than say a teacher, pastor, or prophet, so if this evangelist shared in the ministry with other qualified elders with different gifts, a much broader base of wisdom and truth will be provided for all. The teacher will learn the importance of evangelism from the evangelist. The evangelist will discover greater depths of knowledge from the prophet or teacher, and so on; and, in general, everyone will benefit from the spiritual gift of others. "As every man has received the gift, even so minister one to another as good stewards of the manifold grace of God." (I Peter 4:10.)

Ideally the church should have a plural ministry of those with various spiritual gifts, who have attained to the qualifications of leadership, ministering to the congregation. Does this mean that a younger believer perhaps less than qualified is not free to minister his spiritual gift? No. I believe there is evidence from Scripture that these younger less mature Christians would have freedom to minister their gift to others, but perhaps in a less active or authoritative capacity. Their insights would be brought more under the oversight and discernment of the elders. "Ye younger, submit yourselves unto the elder." (I Peter 5:5.)

In this book I would like to avoid going into the subject of spiritual gifts. I believe this subject has been one of much attention by Christian teachers for years now. But rather I would like to look into this subject of qualifications of elders or leaders from Titus and I Timothy, a less tasteful topic, one that

we hear seldomly discussed today.

I think one of the main reasons we hear qualifications less commonly addressed today than spiritual gifts is because they are not simply achieved. One cannot pay his tuition at a Bible school and come away in three or four years with a degree in the Godly home and marriage. God intended for these qualifications to be this way, because He wanted us to put into leadership those who had been a product of His transforming grace, built up in practical Biblical wisdom, and consistently manifesting this wisdom and grace for a long period of time. We cannot simply master these qualities through intellectual study; they must be built in our daily lives through the transforming power of God's grace. We cannot easily pretend to have these qualities.

- Some Qualifications for Leadership from I Timothy 3 and Titus -

As we begin to look into these two passages of Scripture, our goal is to extract a basic description of the character of the Christian man involved. This discussion is not intended to be exhaustive on these particular passages, but more as useful guidelines in evaluating others in leadership, and in evaluating the progress of our own spiritual growth towards leadership. I would say that it is probably more important for the man who is aspiring to or desiring a position of leadership in the church or any position of Christian ministry to use this list for self evaluation.

Consider the list, make an honest current appraisal of one's self, and then either go ahead and take the lead, or perhaps wait and give the Lord more time to perfect some of the areas that appear a little deficient.

I realize that not every Christian man is necessarily to be one of the leaders in the church; some may not "desire the office of a bishop", but I think this should probably be a spiritual objective for far more men than what is generally encouraged today. It would certainly be a Godly objective for a Christian man to be

working towards these qualifications in his own life and as a leader in his own home, or in preparing for Christian service in some other capacity. Not all men are to be leaders in the church, but they are to be leaders in their own homes.

Indeed, one of the most profound failures of the traditional church system as we know it today is that it rarely leaves any room or gives any encouragement for a Christian man to aspire to or work towards a place of spiritual leadership in the church. In fact, the traditional policy of trying to hire one man to be the leader and teacher of a group in very principle actually precludes and stunts the spiritual aspirations of the men in the group. The church system as we know it is at least another part of the reason we are hearing the cry, "Where are the men in spiritual leadership today?!" By returning to a plural leadership, making it available to the laity, coupled with allowing for the ministry of individual spiritual gifts by those of true Biblical qualification, we will soon experience a renewal of quantity and quality of spiritual leadership in our churches. I would urge churches to return to this approach in selecting church leadership as the early church precedent describes.

- Qualifications Described -

In both passages, I Tim. 3 and Titus 1, Paul begins with the statement that such an aspiring leader must be blameless, and then he goes into a description of specific character. I feel that what Paul is saying is that in order for a man to have character that is above reproach (blameless), he must have his life fairly closely in line with this subsequent list of qualities.

The first topic addressed in both letters is the issue of a man's marriage; he must be "the husband of one wife". This at first glance would appear rather simple for most Christians to comply with today; our laws do not allow polygamy. Some would teach that this phrase is not actually addressing the subject of polygamy, but rather the issue of remarriage. A man was not to be a leader if he was divorced and remarried. But wouldn't this phrase also include a man who was a widower

and then remarried? Certainly being a remarried widower wouldn't disqualify a man for a leadership position. I do feel that if a Christian couple's marriage ends in divorce and the man remarries, that it would be certainly questionable whether he should take a leadership position. My feeling is that he would be disqualified in keeping with this passage.

But there is more to this little phrase of "the husband of one wife" than meets the eye. This phrase, I believe, actually sets the basis for describing the moral character of this man, and I believe Paul is also simply asking, "Does this man have an exemplary marriage?"

Some believe polygamy was practiced in Paul's day; it was acceptable. Many were probably doing it. "What was wrong with this?" they would say. But for a Christian man, it was a clear violation of conscience and not to be justified, even in light of their present social norms. Similarly there are many practices in our present society which are a clear violation of the Christian's conscience, or at least they should be. I was recently reading about a couple who came to Christ in America in 1790. They had slaves prior to their conversion like everyone else, but as soon as they came to Christ they immediately freed their slaves. It became an obvious violation of moral conscience for them to continue to keep them; but not all Christians felt this way about slavery in 1790. Many socially acceptable practices and norms of our present society should also be a clear violation of conscience for the Christian, especially a Christian leader.

The world around us does many things that as a Christian man desiring a position of leadership, he should be clearly opposed to. Some may question me on this point, but I personally feel that owning a TV is one of those socially acceptable practices that, for a Christian leader, should be a violation of conscience. Through having one, this example to the congregation not only could embolden a weaker brother to follow along, but it also is a temptation to children. In Paul's day when a Christian man was the husband of one wife, he was firmly saying, "I am not going to mingle with certain practices of

society even if the world around me says it's OK."

This phrase "the husband of one wife" literally means a "one woman sort of a man". In other words, does this aspiring leader have a sense of devotion, commitment, loyalty, and oneness with this one woman, his wife; or does he show interest, inappropriate friendliness, other preoccupations, attractions, or improprieties with others? Does he show sensitivity to and avoid certain things like improper greetings (hugging, kissing, etc.), conversation, counseling, and other involvements which might cause jealousy from his own wife or cause others to question his motives. Purity and properness in this area is important. Our modern work environments should be considered with this in mind. This phrase speaks of this man's acquired moral character, and what kind of example he will be to others in this most important area of his life.

From Titus the next area for examination has to do with this man's ability to convey his moral principles to those closest to him— "the husband of one wife, *having faithful children not accused of riot or unruly."* (Titus 1:6.) Here again, this second phrase has far more to it than what meets the eye. First of all this phrase "faithful children" speaks of children who are certainly believers; but more than this, they are living out a consistent (faithful) Christian life. They are steadfastly walking with the Lord. Because, after all, this man desiring to be a leader is going to be teaching others how to walk with Christ on a daily basis; are his own children doing that? If they are not, then there is some question as to whether he will be able to teach others to do the same. "For if a man know not how to rule his own house, how shall he take care of the church of God?" (I Tim. 3:5.)

He is to have "faithful children *not accused of riot or unruly."* This word *riot* has in it the idea of excess, unrestrained, or uncontrolled appetites or lusts; it is describing the moral character of this man's children. Riot can even be seen in younger children simply by observing the younger child's conduct; and again from I Tim. 3:4, they are to be in "subjection with all gravity or dignity." In other words, they are to be proper chil-

dren.

This word *unruly* means not consistently subject to rule; they tend to be rebellious at times. This word is describing the subjective nature of this man's children, their meekness, their quietness, and their responsiveness to authority. Basically what we are to see here in this man's life is an exemplary marriage and family life as well.

It has been a standing joke for years in many fundamental churches that pastor's kids are notably the least behaved children in the church. Paul says it should be just the opposite! Some time ago a pastor from a large, fundamental church visited our home, and he was jokingly talking about the conduct of pastors' children. He said that a pastor friend of his jestingly said, "The reason the pastors' kids are so bad is because they are always playing with the deacons' kids." I believe this is a sad but true critique to the fact that for years we have been selecting leadership in clear violation of Scripture.

What we are actually seeing here in these first two qualities of marriage and child conduct is first this man's moral character and then secondly his ability to teach this character and to maintain proper order and subjection in his home. Because this man is to be an "example to the flock" (I Peter 5:3) his home life is very much a part of this example. Furthermore, most of the challenges that a man will face in leading a church will first be encountered on a smaller scale at home. Therefore, success in his own home comes first.

It will take time for God's transforming power of grace to bring a Christian man to a state of having this Godly character and skill; it cannot happen overnight. Being raised in a Christian home is not sufficient experience either to establish these qualities; it will help, but a man's leadership qualities will need to be first proven in his own marriage and home life. This is why the home schooling movement is so important to Christianity as a whole, because we have thousands of Christian fathers concentrating on their own marriages and homes, learning to rule well in their own homes; this in turn will provide a

future bank of qualified men for church leadership. *We are doing far more than building Godly homes by home schooling— we are laying the foundation for future Godly church assemblies.*

This is also why, from our list of qualifications from I Tim. 3, we find that this man is not to be a *novice,* one who is a new convert, or perhaps one who hasn't passed through enough Christian experience to thoroughly test his skills in leadership or faith (experiences that a man will certainly gain to a large degree if he is being successful in his own home). This word *novice* does not necessarily speak of age or necessarily how long he has been a Christian, though this is certainly part of the consideration; but probably more accurately in this context, he is one who has had sufficient experience to prove his ability to bear the burden of the task ahead without being lifted up with personal pride.

Next I would like to look at this quality of being able or *apt to teach.* Here again a man's home is the place where much of the skill in teaching is to be acquired. A man is going to be hard put to have an exemplary marriage and family if he is unskilled in teaching and applying Scripture. From Ephesians 5:25-27, we observe that the husband is to "sanctify" his wife with the "washing of the Word". This sanctifying of the wife is perhaps one of his first assignments in edifying or exhortation. A newly married man is also instructed from the law to stay home and "cheer up" or encourage his wife. Fathers are next to bring up their children in the "admonition and nurturing" or training and instruction of the Lord's ways. So a Godly Christian father has routinely been involved in counseling, edifying, exhorting, encouraging, admonishing, training, and instructing in his own home. This plays a major role in this man being apt to teach in the church. Of course, further insight and depth of knowledge was gained through sitting under other elders who have labored in the "Word and doctrine." (I Tim. 5:17.) Paul instructed Timothy to pass on his teachings to "faithful" men who would be able, in turn, to "teach others also." (II Tim. 2:2.)

So we have here a man who has spent many hours in Bible instruction and counseling in his own home; he has also gained

insight from sitting under other elders and teachers. In addition to this, he has certainly spent many, many hours meditating in Scripture which would include the apostles' doctrines; all of this combined training has brought him to the place of being "apt to teach".

Next let us consider this quality of being *vigilant*. This is basically being circumspectful. He has gained much of this quality from carefully looking over the concerns of his household, especially spiritual concerns. He has carefully made a personal study of the little details in the Christian walk of his own family and has ministered God's solutions to these concerns. Protection is also very much a part of this quality, and spiritual protection begins in the home and then is transferred to the church body as a whole.

From here we come to a list of individual words taken collectively from I Tim. 3 and Titus. These words outline a basic personality/character description that has been acquired in this man's life through the transforming power of grace. This list includes such words as: not self willed, not soon angry, not given to wine, no striker, not given to filthy lucre, not covetous, sober, just, holy, temperate, etc. Some of these words are somewhat self explanatory; others could be expounded upon. For example, soberness could suggest one who has an even keel in his emotions. He does not allow his emotions to run his life or affect his discernment; he is sober. Not that he is void of enthusiasm, but just that he has the ability to rule his spirit. A man who cannot rule his spirit can be more easily misled or drawn away into fair sounding error or teachings. "He that has no rule over his spirit is like a city broken down, and without walls (defense)." (Prov. 25:28.)

This word sober along with several others in this list basically describe a self controlled man, self control that has been a product of transforming grace. For example "soberness" speaks of self control in the area of one's emotions or spirit. "Not given to wine" speaks of acquired self control in the area of fleshly appetites or indulgences. "No striker and no brawler" give a description of acquired self control over a sudden burst of

anger (no striker), or as in the case of a brawler, having harbored anger or having a defensive, contentious spirit toward those that disagree with him.

"Not greedy of filthy lucre" would speak of self control in the area of money or other kinds of personal gain such as fame or recognition. "Not covetous" would fall into a similar category of having no personal greed or the desire to possess or control others for personal gain, or to promote an organization for personal recognition. Sometimes discipleship can become a form of coveting or an attempt to possess followers rather than for the proper motive of wanting to build up followers of Christ. Rather a leader should "not be self willed."

Furthermore the wives of such leaders should have also acquired evidence of self control in such areas as the tongue. They are not to be "slanderous" or "malicious talkers or gossips". (I Tim. 3:11.) But instead they have become "teachers of good things". They also have experienced the power of grace to transform similar areas in their life such as "not given to wine" (thus controlling fleshly appetites) and "soberness" (controlling emotions or their spirit).

So we see described in these two passages a leader and his wife who have acquired victory through grace over such areas as greed, fleshly appetites, anger, the tongue, their emotions, personal ambitions, and so on. This very accurately describes a man who has "fallen into the earth and died" to self. This kind of transformation cannot happen quickly; it will take years of time for a man and his wife to acquire these Godly qualities. God meant for mature Christians to be in a place of leadership in the Church.

Isn't it encouraging to realize that most of this Godly character needed for church leadership will be first encountered and learned as we simply go about the business of building a Godly marriage and home? There are no crash courses or classrooms where we can be enrolled that can give us lasting victory over these areas described here in I Tim. 3 and Titus. This kind of transformation cannot be acquired mentally or through personal effort. This kind of character will need to be built into our

lives over a period of time by the power of grace; there are no short cuts.

Certainly much of this acquired character will be seen by those in the world around us. "Moreover he must be of good reputation with those who are without." (I Tim. 3:7.) This not only describes this man's apparent character, but I believe it is also describing this man's ability to serve, and what kind of servant he will be within the church. Generally success and a good report or reputation is acquired by the diligent and conscientious servant, and this will be evidenced to a large degree by this man's performance in the secular world or work environment, those who are outside of Christian circles.

I think it is somewhat obvious from the above descriptions that a Christian leader who is ministering his gift to other believers should show ample evidence of being transformed by God's grace though the working of the Holy Spirit and the washing of Christ's blood. We realize that this is a high standard, maybe even idealistic, but it's a goal that Paul has set up for aspiring leaders to be working towards and for present leaders to use as a personal check list for areas that need improvement.

Finally and above all, he is a man of pure speech and a pure heart, "holding the mystery of the faith in a pure conscience" (I Tim. 3:9), and he is able to communicate the "mystery of Godliness" which he has achieved to a good degree in his own life. He is now prepared to communicate by his example and words this purity and Godliness to others as a leader in the church or in some other capacity of Christian service.

- Elders and Deacons -

The early church had basically two leadership positions; they were the elders and the deacons. These men were the ministers in the New Testament church. The elders generally did the bulk of the teaching, and perhaps one of these elders was conisdered the Senior Elder or Superintendent of the church as noted earlier.

The Scriptures also give us a qualification description for the leadership position of deacons. I personally believe these men were "elders in training", perhaps younger men of noble character who were doing a good job in their own homes as well. "Let the deacons be the husbands of one wife, ruling their children and their own houses well." (I Tim. 3:12.) The quality of being "able to teach" is absent from the list for deacons, so perhaps they were not the regular teachers of the group as yet; perhaps this function was left more to the elders. We do know that Stephen, traditionally known as one of the deacons of the Jerusalem church, was a man full of wisdom and the Holy Ghost (Acts 6). When he was interrogated by the Counsel, he was falsely accused of "speaking blasphemous words" (Acts 6:11, 13). Evidently he had been doing some public preaching, and, of course, his sermon to the Sanhedrin was a notable discourse of Biblical wisdom (Acts 7). So deacons may at least play a part in the speaking and teaching ministry of the church.

Phillip, also one of the deacons from Acts 6, was involved in evangelistic ministry and church planting following the dispersal of the Jerusalem church. Of course, deacons were first chosen to allow the elders (apostles) more time to devote to preaching and prayer by relieving the elders of more minor spiritual duties. Younger men with younger children would most likely fill a position of deacon in the church assembly while training under and working towards an eventual position of elder.

We are following this arrangement in our small assembly. Most often my young married son, Ben, opens our service leading the music and prayer time. Usually he or one of the other young men will have a short Bible teaching, testimony, or some words of edification. Either I or one of the older men in the church will then bring a longer message and teaching. This practice of involving young men of spiritual ability and older men of spiritual maturity to be the ministers in the church, we feel, is following along with the New Testament directives of having elders and deacons in leadership.

- Consider the Outcome of the Lives
of Those in Leadership -

Jesus and Paul both directed the Christian to consider the results, the fruit in the lives, of those in leadership. Paul (I am assuming he was the author of the Hebrew letter) said, "Remember them which have the rule over you, who have spoken unto you the Word of God: whose faith follow (imitate), considering the end (outcome) of their conversation (manner of life)." (Hebrews 13:7.) Paul was assuming that those who were in leadership had commendable, exemplary lives. They had children who were walking with Christ, and they had helped other families to also have success with their homes.

Jesus said you will know good teaching by the fruit in the lives of the teachers. "Beware of false prophets, which come to you in sheep's clothing...Ye shall know them by their fruits." (Matt. 7:15, 16.)

Today we are being warned that making such an evaluation constitutes some kind of judgmentalism, but both Jesus and Paul urge the Christian to use such discernment for their own protection and well-being. The adversary wants to keep the Christian off guard and from using discernment, and if he can make one feel guilty for being discerning by labeling discernment as judging, he will keep the Christian in a state of vulnerability. It is vitally important that the Christian carefully discerns the lives of those over him, not to the point of being nit-picking or fault finding or judgmental, but there is the need to identify major concerns that you see in the life of those in leadership. Don't feel guilty with this; it is part of being a responsible parent and Christian.

I know of some in leadership who voluntarily removed themselves (temporarily or sometimes permanently) from a teaching position when problems in their own homes or personal life began to surface. Far too often today, we hear Christians in leadership making excuses or growing quiet over sons or daughters who have gotten into wrong music, have moral problems, have rebelled, left home, gotten divorces, or in other ways

shown signs of departing from the faith. These warning signs should not be taken lightly; if the leader has failed in his own home, he will likely mislead others to some extent.

By carefully following Paul's directives for selecting leadership, choosing men of maturity and sufficient age to show the outcome of their faith, we will be much more likely to select reliable leadership.

- The Christian Woman's Role in Ministry -

Today the church often misses an important function of the Christian woman in ministering to the needs of the other sisters or younger sisters in the church. We are seeing women being ordained to pastorships, assuming a position designated for Christian men, or in other similar contexts where they are teaching men in mixed group situations. Women teaching in such capacities is contrary to Scripture. "But I suffer not a woman to teach or to usurp authority over the man." (I Tim. 2:12.) But on the other hand, Titus says "the aged (older) women" were to be "teachers of good things...that they may teach the young women to be sober, to love their husbands, to love their children, to be discreet, chaste, keepers at home, good, obedient to their own husbands, that the Word of God be not blasphemed (or maligned)." (Titus 2:3,4,5.) God never intended for the woman to be out front taking a leadership or teaching position in the church assembly or any other mixed Christian setting; but they were to work quietly and hiddenly in a capacity of counsel and comfort to younger Christian women in such areas as the marriage relationship and child training and in a supportive role to their husband's ministry and life.

I Tim. 3 gives a description of some qualities to be found in this woman's life. Certainly the wife who is assuming such a position of counselor to other women was the wife of a leader who has himself met the proper qualifications for leadership. He has ministered to and sanctified his own wife, and she in turn now has some skill in being able to minister to other women; the early church relied heavily on this counseling position of the older Christian women.

Today due to the influence of the social practices of our society around us, this counseling position is often given to a pastor or a "professional" male counselor, and men counseling other women many times are open to much temptation. Early church leadership wisely avoided the potential temptations of this by following the directives in Titus where the older women counseled the younger, especially younger married women.

A recent study by a leading university in California discovered that the greatest force of attraction (even greater than outward attractiveness, dress, hair style, make-up or anything else) between a man and woman was caused by the sharing of heart felt conversation or concerns. This type of intimate communication more than any other single factor led to a relationship developing between a man and a woman. This is what transpires during counseling. These Scriptures designating the older women as counselors to the younger women wisely and properly presented the most Godly solution to this possible problem.

Paul wisely not only gives directives for the man in leadership, but also for this man's wife, because Paul recognized the valuable function a wife would have as counselor which would also protect the holiness and purity of those in the church. I basically see church leadership as a co-ministry of an elder or deacon and his wife ministering to others together. Aquilla and Priscilla are never mentioned separately in Scripture (they ministered together), and we know they had a church in their house (perhaps in two different localities at different times). Paul was very close with this couple. He had even worked with them for a period of time, and they certainly understood Paul's directives for ministry. Aquilla and Priscilla together pulled Apollos aside and "expounded unto him the way of God more perfectly." (Acts 18:26.)

I would urge Christian couples to diligently seek the ministry the Lord has for your lives together. Whether it be a church in your home, a fellowship, a Bible study, a ministry in writing, or a ministry to the body of Christ in some other way, God is looking for this kind of team ministry where husbands and wives together are first determined to build a Godly home, and then desiring to begin ministering to others as the Lord directs.

Chapter Seven

The Position of Authority in the Church

Today we are seeing more and more emphasis being given to the position of church authority. This is a subject that needs to be accurately understood from a Biblical perspective because since the time of Christ, history gives us an untold number of incidences where church authority has been misused to the detriment of God's people. The great struggle of the Protestant Reformation was a struggle against the clutches of church authority. Martin Luther's "Ninety-five Thesis" became widely known and enabled the common man to see through many of the abuses of church authority. In these he attacked the teaching behind the sale of indulgences which kept the common man committed to the "established" church, and he also attacked the church's preoccupation with materialism and worldliness. The Pilgrim fathers and other Puritans in England had a similar encounter with the established Anglican church; they wanted to purify the church, and if that wasn't possible they were willing to start new ones.

As I have just noted in the previous chapter, church leaders were to be, above all, a Godly example to those in the assembly;

church leadership is, above all, an exampleship position. As long as those designated to a church leadership position meet these qualifications set down in Timothy and Titus, we can be reasonably sure that their ministry will be beneficial to our homes. Association in a church fellowship will be further beneficial when those we are assembling with share a like-mindedness with us in lifestyle and objectives.

But when a church leadership position is acquired on some basis other than Paul's guidelines, and when fellowshipping with others seems to present to us a continual conflict of principles, then assembling in such a situation can become detrimental to the spiritual well being of our home. We can "come together not for the better, but for the worse." (I Cor. 11:17.) So by just arbitrarily putting ourselves under some church's authority certainly doesn't guarantee our spiritual well being.

Church authority is an important function because God designed it and established it for the protection and nurturing of the younger, less experienced Christian. Church leaders were to be able to "watch for the souls" (Heb. 13:17) of those in their assembly just as a father would carefully watch for the souls of his own children. But children are not to always be children; they are to grow up to the point of maturity so that they can make wise choices in being able to protect their own lives and their own future families. In the same way, Christians are to grow up in Christ and become "no more children tossed to and fro" (Eph. 4:14) by every new teaching that comes along. God expects Christians to grow to a point of maturity and discernment that will enable them to make the right choices in life.

I can see this in my own sons. Near the age of twenty, they came to a point of maturity in which they could make wise decisions in life. Of course, I was there for counsel and direction, but I felt it was time for them to make some choices; I couldn't make them for them. They sought my counsel just as I would seek counsel of others in my life, but we men individually have the obligation to ultimately consider how Christ is leading; our counselor cannot make that estimate clearly for

us. Counsel from an authority should be highly considered, but ultimately the head of every man should be Christ, not another person, once this man has reached maturity.

The church system as we know it today tends to lock Christians into a childhood type maturity. The ultimate headship of Christ over a man's life is many times discouraged, and we don't teach men with the objective in mind that they will in time be able to teach others. "The things that thou hast heard of me...the same commit thou to faithful men who shall be able to teach others also." (II Timothy 2:2.) We have more of a system where those in the congregation are to remain like children and to remain students, and they are never expected to come to a place of being teachers themselves ("Ye ought to be teachers..."– Heb. 5:12) or at least to work toward a position of leadership.

Bible schools have reduced the position of church leadership to a profession that is acquired through academic study and graduation rather than a position that a Christian man ascends to or matures into. The early church had a continual flow of new leadership budding and maturing who could in time either move into a position of leadership or be qualified to start their own church. We have deviated from this earlier precedent.

Today we hold in high esteem men of God from the past, such notables as: Charles Spurgeon, D. L. Moody, Charles Finney, John Bunyan, Francis Asbury, and many others; but few Christians realize that these men were all either self taught preachers or had learned their skills and knowledge through working closely with other ministers...they were not college trained for the ministry. They were not ordained of men, but they were ordained of God. There have always been times in history when God has raised up His own ministers to meet the spiritual needs of His people. For example, in the great Methodist-Baptist Revival in America during the mid 1700's, many an untrained (not institutionally trained) frontier preacher took the spiritual lead of a congregation. "Methodist circuit-riders such as Francis Asbury inspired many a boy to feel called to preach

as he listened to the gospel in a barn or tavern." (*Eerdman's Handbook,* p. 534.)

In *The Journal and Letters of Francis Asbury* it is pointed out that Francis himself was a self taught preacher; he learned his skills in preaching and grew in Biblical discernment through sitting under John Wesley's teaching, personal study, and by reading the writings of other notable Christian men. His only formal schooling was from the age of six or seven to the age of thirteen at a nearby school in England. "He was so apt in his studies that he could read the Bible at the age of six or seven." From the age of thirteen to eighteen, he apprenticed with a blacksmith, a work that developed his physical constitution to equip him for the strenuous tasks he would face as an American wilderness circuit riding preacher. But this informally trained preacher had an enormous impact on American moral character. "As a bearer of a moral culture and its civilizing consequences to the frontier settlements of America, Francis Asbury has no peer (equal) in history."

It is noted that "his preachers, most of whom had little formal education, went into every new community and nearly every log cabin in the wilderness. They fought intemperance and every form of wrongdoing; and they made Godly, law-respecting citizens out of people who might otherwise have been ruffians. Asbury preached a gospel of personal salvation, as did all others in his day." (Above quotations from *The Journal and Letters of Francis Asbury,* Vol 1, page X, published by Abingdon Press.)

The Methodist church was the largest denomination by the mid 1800's, followed by the growing Baptist movement. "The Baptists appealed particularly to the lower middle class. Their untrained and unpaid farmer-ministers would gather a few families around them and organize a church." (*Eerdman's Handbook,* p. 535.)

Note how both of these denominations started out with untrained and unlearned men (from a collegiate perspective), but they were very well trained from a practical perspective of Godliness and unquestionable standards of purity. By modern

standards, these early American pioneers of church planting and leadership would have been dubbed unqualified or unorthodox, but they brought about a renewal and revival of Christian virtue and holiness to the church at large that may never again be equaled in America.

The point I am trying to make by the above examples is that a man can become quite capable to lead a Christian group without following the traditional methods of preparing for church leadership. There are many home schooling moms today who have acquired a great degree of skill and ability to lead a home school without going to teacher's college; in fact, statistics are showing that many are actually doing a much better job than their public or private school counterpart.

Does this mean that I am against Bible schools? Actually, no, there is always benefit when we spend a concentrated time of study in God's word, provided that it is taught properly. I am only saying that this study does not necessarily prepare one to be a church leader. The qualifications listed in the previous chapter describe a great degree of experience and the living out of God's Word in daily life over a period of time in preparation for leadership.

James says, "Be doers of the Word and not hearers only, deceiving yourselves." It is quite easy for head knowledge to deceive a person into thinking they actually understand and are living out Scripture. James goes on to say that if we "continue" in the Word, bringing it to fruit through experience, we will truly be blessed in our actions and understand the truth of Scripture. (See James 1:22-25.) This is what prepares a man for church leadership, and this preparation should be acquired through applying Scripture in daily life and experience.

- Church Leadership: Exampleship or Lordship? -

The Scriptures clearly describe a church authority position given to church leaders, but just how far reaching is this position of authority, and how much control do these men have over the lives of others in the congregation? As we have noted, there was a plural leadership in the N.T. churches. In Acts,

Chapter 15, we see that when controversial matters arose, they were discussed by this plurality of leadership, and decisions were arrived at accordingly with perhaps one leader (James) summarizing the consensus of opinion. This is a clear example of the Jerusalem elders acting for the spiritual protection of those under them. They were "watching for the souls" (Heb. 13:17) of the younger Christian brothers.

This is an important function of the elders, and this promotes and protects sound doctrine. It is fairly easy for a younger, less experienced and less knowledgeable Christian to come to wrong conclusions on certain Biblical concepts. For this reason, Paul urges the Christian to look into the lifestyle and fruit of the elders' or leaders' family, marriage, and general character in determining leadership ability as I have said in the preceding chapter. If the leader clearly has these qualities, then the younger, less experienced Christian should accordingly "submit themselves to the elder." (I Peter 5:5.)

However, even though the younger are to submit to the elder, it is vitally important that this younger Christian man doesn't become a follower or disciple of another man. The younger Christian is to become a follower of Christ (Christ's disciple), holding ultimately to the headship (ultimate authority) of Christ, not another man. Paul chided the Colossian church for allowing others to become their ultimate authority (head) "and not holding the head" (Col. 2:19) or the ultimate headship of Christ over their lives. When leadership authority goes beyond and takes the headship of Christ over a Christian man, then they are exerting too much control or authority.

Even the Apostle Paul was very careful not to go beyond the headship of Christ in another Christian man's life. Paul praised the Corinthian believers for keeping the teaching that he had passed on to them, but he also wanted them to keep in mind that their ultimate authority (or head) was Christ, not himself, Paul, a man. "Follow my example as I follow the example of Christ. I praise you for remembering me in everything and for holding to the teaching, just as I passed them on to you." (I Cor. 11: 1, 2.) But then the apostle goes on to urge the brothers not

to become "Paulites" or followers of men, but to be followers of the ultimate headship of Christ. "But I would have you know, that the head of every man is Christ: and the head of the woman is the man..." (I Cor. 11:3.)

From here in this passage of Scripture, Paul goes into a discussion of the "dishonoring" towards Christ that takes place in a Christian man's life when he places so much authority or puts so much power in another man's authority over himself that he shames his own head. In a sense, this man gives so much glory or authority to another man rather than to Christ who was and is to be his ultimate authority, that he dishonors his head. Paul says that this man feels "shameful" like he would if he had long hair or his head covered. On the other hand, the woman was cautioned not to allow her "head" to be "uncovered" or out from under the spiritual discernment and protection of the man. (It is our personal conviction that the Scriptures here are describing the necessity of a spiritual covering and not necessarily a physical covering. For more details on this subject, please see Chapter Eight.)

Today we are seeing more and more teaching along the lines of church authority, and there is certainly a place for sound men in leadership as examples to the flock and as wise teachers of truth and virtue, but these men are not to be intermediaries between other men and Christ. They are *not* to assume a position of lordship or headship or priestship over the other brothers. It is sometimes difficult to sense when men are "lording" it over one another. Church authority should be approached cautiously today because church leadership can very easily drift from an exampleship position into a priesthood position; this is really what happened with the Roman Catholic religion and the early church. For this reason the younger brothers should be urged to constantly be keeping their head as Christ, not another man.

The Bereans are a good example of men who understood this concept of Christ's headship. They willingly received what Paul had to say, but they were not going to allow this to take the place of God's ultimate guidance in their lives. "Now the Bereans

were of more noble character than the Thessalonians, for they received the message with great eagerness and examined the Scriptures every day to see if what Paul said was true." (See Acts 17:11.) They wanted God to directly confirm Paul's teaching from the Word; their head remained Christ. Christ and the apostles in numerous passages cautioned the believer of the dangers of allowing church leadership to become a lordship type of ministry. "But Jesus called his disciples unto him, and said, 'Ye know that the princes of the Gentiles exercise dominion over them, and they that are great exercise authority upon them. But it shall not be so among you.'" (Matt 20:25, 26. Compare also Mark 10:42.) Jesus warned that there would be some in leadership who take satisfaction in being "called of men, Rabbi, Rabbi (Teacher or Master-teacher). But be not ye called Rabbi (Master): for one is your Master, even Christ (the headship of Christ); and all ye are brethren." (Matt. 23:7,8.)

Paul warned the Ephesian elders that "even from their own number, men will arise (exalt themselves, taking authority) in order to draw away disciples after them." (Acts 20:30.) Peter pointed out that leaders were not to be "lords" or to take the headship of Christ, but to rather be "examples to the flock." "Neither as being lords over God's heritage, but examples to the flock." (I Peter 5:3.)

There are some who take such passages as found in Hebrews 13:7 and 17, "Obey them and remember them that have the rule over you", as Biblical evidence that the apostles taught a lordship or headship type of authority position for church leaders. But how do we reconcile this with the above sited passages that seem to warn against this? A careful study of this word "rule" gives one the idea of this leader being a "guide to follow," or a leader or shepherd going ahead of the sheep and thus being an example to imitate or follow—not someone who has the capacity to dictate, rule over, or take absolute authority. The margin of the authorized version indicates these men "are the guides". A translation of Hebrews 13:7 would accurately be, "Be mindful of the example of them which are the guides over you who have spoken unto you the Word of God, whose faith

(or example) imitate, and observe attentively the outcome of their manner of life." The younger were to carefully study and copy the example of the elder, but their head was to remain Christ.

One of the great struggles of the Protestant reformers was to restore to the common Christian man the headship or sovereignty of Christ over their lives. Some teaching today on church authority has turned the exampleship position of Christian leadership back into such a headship position; in a very real sense, many churches have fallen back into the same pattern of the pre-Reformation days. In many instances, Christians have unknowingly, and sometimes consciously, designated certain Christian men as their master (or teacher), becoming followers of men; we have created to some degree a protestant priesthood out of church leadership. Church leadership is often erroneously equated with governmental or parental authority. Although well intentioned, this authority role designated to church leadership is creating a priesthood, lordship type of function out of the pastorate, and Paul certainly didn't teach this; in fact, he warned against it!

- Maintaining Order By Submitting To Elders -

In keeping with Scripture we believe it is important to encourage submission to elders in an assembly to preserve order and properness and sound doctrine. The younger and others should respectfully submit to the requests and admonition of these elders. Elders are not infallible, and, of course, the Word of God is the ultimate source on issues of debate. But just as in a household, final decisions must be made by someone to preserve unity and maintain harmony. Therefore, it is important to allow a ruling or senior elder to make final decisions after sufficient discussion and consideration has been given to various issues encountered from time to time. Others should cheerfully submit to such decisions and to trust that God is working through this elder even if his decision varies from their views or feelings. This is best to maintain peace and harmony.

Decisions of the elders may be respectfully appealed, but some kind of authority structure is necessary in any organization to maintain orderliness. The elders are available for counsel, and they may also in a spirit of encouragement make suggestions to individuals or the church body as a whole that will enhance the holiness and constructive fruitfulness of the group. Therefore the Word of God coupled with wise Biblical and spiritual discernment of the elders allowing one elder to make the final decisions will generally lead to unity and peace.

- Qualifications Build Examples, Not Lords -

Many Christians today have failed to recognize that church leadership is the only authority position in Scripture that has "qualifications." (See I Tim. 3 & Titus.) In Scripture, we are commanded to obey the king regardless of his ability as king. We are "to be ready to every good work." (Titus 3:1.) Kings and governmental authorities were to be obeyed, in general, regardless of their qualifications, provided that, what they are asking us to do is a "good work". In other words, if the authorities command us to stop preaching the Gospel, we will need to "obey God rather than men." It would not be a "good work" in God's sight to stop preaching the Gospel. Similarly, in Moses' day, the mid wives were told by the government (Pharaoh) to slay the male babies that were born, but they feared God (God is the greater authority to be obeyed) and rejected the Pharaoh's command because they knew it was obviously not a "good work" that the government was asking of them; and you will recall that God blessed the mid wives even though they deliberately disobeyed the government. But in general, we are to obey the government, regardless of the qualifications or moral character of those in leadership; there is not a specific list of qualities given for evaluating governmental authority. The Scriptures do indicate that men groan under ungodly governmental leadership, but subjection is still encouraged in general.

Children in Christian homes are to obey their parents "in all

things", regardless of the ability or qualifications of their parents. We find no list of qualifications for parents in Scripture. Similarly Christian wives are to submit to their husbands in everything, in general, regardless of the ability or qualification of their own husbands. But church leaders were first to be "tried" or "proven" before they were to be followed; they were to show clear evidence that they measured up to the qualifications given for men in leadership from I Tim. 3 & Titus. The reason for this basic difference between this leadership (authority) position and all the rest is that church leaders were above all to be "examples to the flock". They were not put in a position to decree, dictate, or "lord" it over the flock or congregation, and as I pointed out earlier there was usually a plurality of leadership rather than a single man over the church. The Apostle Paul even stated that he did not have lordship (translated dominion) over the faith of other Christians: "Not that we have dominion over your faith but are helpers of your joy." (II Cor. 1:24.)

God will work through church leaders in a counseling position, but a church leader doesn't just arbitrarily or automatically have "good" counsel. The quality of a church leader's counsel or teaching will be in proportion to this man meeting the qualifications previously described. But church counsel should never take the place of the ultimate authority or headship of Christ in a Christian man's life, and far too frequently today church leadership counsel is often given greater weight than the counsel a Christian man will have from his own wife or the authority the man has in his own home. Scriptures indicate the extreme value of the wife in this counseling position in marriage (See our book *Becoming Heirs Together of the Grace of Life*). When this counseling function of the wife is set below that of church brethren, too much weight or authority has been given to this position of church leadership counsel. Furthermore when church leadership counsel usurps the prompting and leading a man has in a clear conscience from Christ, then too much power has also been given to this church authority position.

It seems ironic to me that at the very time that many are beginning to question the example that church leadership at large is presenting to the family in America, we are beginning to hear the cry, "We must be under church authority." I believe our adversary recognizes the potential moral and spiritual damage that many churches present today, and he is going to attempt to promote a sense of obligation for the Christian to be tied to such churches. Many home schooling families are setting and living a much higher moral standard than what is available and presented at the traditional church setting. If we can be falsely made to think we are not properly "under" church authority, we will be tempted to sit under this influence. We must insist on and begin to establish a higher standard; it will be for the true glory of God.

- The Woman's Place Under Authority -

For the woman, we find somewhat of a different set of principles in regards to authority. The woman is directed to have her head as the man and not Christ or another brother or leader in the Church. The head of the woman (wife and daughter) is the man (or her husband or father, respectively). (I Cor. 11:2 and also from Eph. 5:23 "For the husband is the head of the wife. . . ") Today there is a deviation from this principle being promoted in Christian circles. Much of this has probably resulted from the co-educational classroom and lifestyle of American society where women have sat in equal capacity with men in most situations. In the early church and the N. T. church setting, Paul says that "if the woman was to learn anything they should ask their husbands at home." (I Cor. 14:35.) Paul assumed there was a headship function of each man in the congregation over their own wives and daughters on spiritual matters. Wives were not to adopt spiritual principles or teaching or express them to others without it first being passed through the discernment and protection of their husband's headship; it was dishonoring and shameful for a woman to do

so. "A woman praying or prophesying with her head uncovered (spiritually) dishonored her head (her own husband)." (See I Cor. 11:5.) This practice, Paul points out, is against the obvious principles of nature, the very way God designed things. "Doth not even nature itself teach you, that if a man have long hair (his head covered) it is a shame unto him? But if a woman have long hair, it is a glory to her; for her hair is given her for a covering." (I Cor. 11:14, 15.)

It is a beautiful, glorious thing when a wife or daughter values and respects the position of headship (covering) designated to her husband or father. This is truly a blessed place for the woman. Not that a woman doesn't have access to Christ through prayer and the presence of the Holy Spirit in her life but just that such access (prayer) or expression of spiritual insight (prophecy) should not be done with disregard or lack of consideration for what her head would be approving. "But every woman that prayeth or prophesieth with her head uncovered dishonereth her head." (I Cor. 11:5.)

I believe that the Christian society at large would be far more blessed today if we would begin returning to this structure of spiritual authority and protection that Paul prescribed. No preaching, teaching, or leadership directives in the church should be issued so strongly that a woman's allegiance to her own husband's or father's authority (feelings, discernment, etc.) should be disregarded, slighted, or challenged. I recognize that much teaching is made today with a disregard for these principles, and it is causing disruption in home authority structure and often causes independence or even rebellion in women. By returning to these principles of headship for both husbands and wives, we not only will be greatly strengthening the unity of marriages and homes, but this is also a necessary prerequisite for the strong and Godly church assembly.

- Children Under Authority -

The authority structure of the home is made complete when children remain in their proper place under their own parents.

Most of us home schooling parents have recognized how the government schools and Christian schools have attempted to take our place of authority over our children. A very subtle, less recognizable source of this authority usurping often takes place in church programming, but it can be just as detrimental. It often starts out as Sunday school or nursery care, and I think some flexibility should be given here for smaller children; it may be appropriate for them to be occupied with some simple coloring papers or such or occasional nursery care. But as children grow older, Sunday school should be approached cautiously.

Allegiance, respect, and loyalty can readily begin to shift from the parents to another source of authority. We did not use a nursery for our little ones, and we avoided Sunday school when our children were younger. Of course, in our home assembly neither of these seemed needful. Each family responsibly takes care of their own children. The children have been taught to sit quietly with their parents, and we have also at the same time tried to "remember their frame" and have not made our church services overly long so that it would make it too difficult for young children to bear.

- The Teen Group -

Many teen groups are designed to supposedly motivate young people, but I think that the young people who actually end up getting motivated in their spiritual life are usually the ones who have parents that have a vision or motivation to serve the Lord themselves. This is somewhat of a difficult area to draw an absolute conclusion for or against such teen training situations. For some youth whose parents are either unbelieving or nominally following the faith, perhaps God would use a teen program to help steer this young person in proper Biblical directions. In some situations an alternative source of authority is needful and useful. But on the other hand, teen groups can sometimes become a source that draws young people away from homes where the parent is taking or would take a

responsible role in shaping their children's spiritual life. The youth group many actually cause disloyalty to the home in this case.

Furthermore, I see the temptations that the co-ed youth group can bring into a young person's life. Those situations which could arouse such youthful passions were to be avoided by the young person. "Flee also youthful lusts." (I Tim. 2:22.) It is rather easy to cause young people to become discontent with their own homes. Social dependency in youth is a common problem in many large church groups. By allowing for interaction of a family with other families rather than breaking up into age segregated groups, much of this can be avoided.

Some other opportunities for young people to get acquainted can be provided. One group we met with for a while had a Friday night "Sing" every so often where a parent or parents along with their teens met together for some fellowship and singing. But this was more of a situation where families were getting together instead of teens going off alone. Many home schooling parents today are questioning the validity of teen groups. Approach this vigilantly and wisely. I think it would be wise to err on the side of being too conservative rather than being too liberal in this area.

Personally our children have never been involved in a youth group or youth programs where young people are routinely involved with each other away from the authority and proximity of their own parents. We feel the best environment for young people to get acquainted is when families are together with other families. This minimizes the temptations of independence which can lead to rebellion; it also helps prevent a "dating spirit" and other youthful temptations from arising. For more information on preparing sons and daughters for courtship and marriage, we have an indepth article on this subject available at a minimal cost through Parable Publishing House.

- Summary of Proper Authority Positions -

This issue of fathers, wives, and children being under proper

authority is actually what sets the house type church or smaller assembly above the rest. In most church settings, fathers are expected to submit to church leadership without considering the qualifications of such leaders and without emphasis being placed on this man's "head" or ultimate authority remaining Christ. Wives are often expected to be subject to church leaders (such as pastors) without regarding the absolute importance of the headship (covering) of their husbands over their lives. And very often children and teens are placed in situations or groups where they are expected to be subject to a substitute authority on a regular basis. Of course, the discerning parent can see that this kind of church environment will disrupt the unity of their home life. Careful attention to proper authority positions for each member of each individual family will be found to be an important aspect to building and maintaining a Godly home and church.

Chapter Eight

Spiritual Warfare and Being Under Proper Authority

This issue of being under proper authority structure is not only essential for maintaining unity in the home, but a disregard for proper arrangement under authority will lead to spiritual struggles. Unfortunately what is happening today is that many Christians are being urged and taught to over–value one authority position above another of higher rank, and this many times leads to an individual finding themselves out from under a God–ordained authority.

The Scriptures over and over again urge the Christian to be subject to authorities in their life. The word used for "subject" is the Greek word "hupotasso" which means to arrange under or to set in array under, similar to the way the army officers of different rank are arrayed under each other. For example, the sergeant would be under the lieutenant; the lieutenant is under the captain who is under the colonel who is under the major, who are all under the general. In the Scripture, we have many authority positions of varying rank; for example, children are to be under parental authority; wives are to be under the husband's authority. There are the elements of governmental authority, church authority, and occupational authority; and finally there

is the authority or ultimate headship of Christ in our lives.

The problem we have today on teaching on authority is that many times we are giving one authority of lesser rank greater value than another of greater rank. It would be like someone trying to assert that a lieutenant or captain has greater rank than a major, to the point where the major's request would be undermined or slighted. When we get authority positions out of rank or order in such a way, individuals will unknowingly find themselves out from under the most important authority in their life. This is what has happened with some teaching on church authority.

The Apostle Paul gives us one vivid example of the ranking of authority in I Cor. 11:3. "But I would have you know that the head of every man is Christ, and the head of the woman is the man, and the head of Christ is God." What we are seeing today is a mis–arrangement of authority being taught. So much power or authority is being given to church authority that it is slighting the essential importance of the man's head (authority) remaining Christ (the man's ultimate authority). Also the church authority position is being ranked above the husband's headship over his wife. What this causes is a man to be out from under the ultimate headship of Christ in his life, and the wife finding herself out from under her husbands's ultimate authority in her life. Whenever we get out from under one authority by overly emphasizing or overly valuing another authority, we end up facing spiritual attack or warfare. In this very chapter (I Cor. 11) where Paul ranks authority positions, he points out that wives are to be careful to keep themselves under their husband's headship to ward off spiritual forces which would include spiritual forces for evil. "For this cause ought the woman to have power (authority) on her head because of the angels." (I Cor. 11:10.)

Many wives, husbands, and children are facing difficulties with rebellion and stress and other troubling situations because they have gotten themselves out from under proper authority due to being subtly encouraged and taught that church leaders have greater authority than they really do. Tempta-

tions children face with misbehavior, independence, rebellion, and other strange abnormalities are many times the result of this mis–arrangement of authority structure. When husbands are removed out from under the headship of Christ, and when wives are slighting the headship of their husbands, then inevitably evil spiritual forces begin attacking everyone in the home in some way. Teen–age rebellion is a vivid and often heart rending result of mistaught authority structure doctrine. When husbands are encouraged to place more "weight" on a brother's or pastor's opinion than drawing from the spiritual counsel of his own wife, then we also end up with a twist in the proper order of our home that will hinder grace.

The wise and discerning Christian leader will take the spiritual authority in the church, being a proper example to the flock, while clearly directing each brother to maintain the headship of Christ in his life; he will also be encouraging wives and daughters to keep themselves under their own husband's and father's spiritual headship and protection. Wives should be urged to "ask their husbands at home" (I Cor. 14:35) in regards to spiritual teaching given in the church, to be sure the teaching is in agreement with their own husband's discernment. Church programming and teaching should not be directed to children in such a way as to cause a lack of allegiance, respect, and loyalty to their father's (and mother's) discernment. We feel Sunday school and children's church often intervenes with this authority structure of the home.

Authority structure is a subject that needs to be properly discerned. History gives us many examples of those who have "crept into houses" and "disrupted whole houses" under the guise of being the "proper" authority to follow. We must be careful not to damage the authority structure of the home by over valuing the authority structure of the church.

- Head Coverings And Being Under Spiritual Authority -

Over the years of our home schooling experience, we have

had opportunities to meet many families which follow certain requirements which they sincerely feel are Scriptural mandates (laws) of Christian conduct such as church ordinances, observances, or regulations. We have run into requirements (laws) in the area of baptism, tithing, observances of the Lord's Supper, this issue of the cloth head covering, and others.

Along the lines of head coverings, I have observed a variety of positions on just what they feel would be the requirements here. Some hold that head coverings are to be only worn during a church service; others would hold that they are certainly to be worn at all times; some feel that the woman's hair should be scrupulously covered to the complete degree; others feel that the woman's hair should be worn long under the covering. Some groups hold that I Cor. 11:15 states that long hair is given to a woman for a covering, and those women who cut their hair short are thus uncovered. Many conservative Christians feel certainly that the issue in I Cor. 11 is purely a spiritual issue and is a discussion of the importance of both wives and daughters being sure they are under their proper spiritual protection or covering, their husband or father.

Although we would respect the convictions of those who feel this passage is describing a physical covering of some kind, our conviction and position would be in line with those who feel and encourage the importance of being under proper spiritual headship or covering. We do not feel that a physical covering is the discussion in this I Cor. 11 passage. Many who hold to the cloth head covering belief will agree or at least concede that the spiritual is important, maybe even more important than the physical; however, there are some concerns that need to be discussed with this issue. First of all, it is important to emphasize that a physical covering will be of no value of protection in the spiritual realm. Many head covering advocates will agree with this statement and assert that the cloth covering is only a symbol of the true spiritual subjection that their wives and daughters should have.

We believe that it would be permissible for wives and daughters to wear physical coverings if they believe or have been

taught that there is some kind of physical covering discussed in this I Cor. 11 passage, *provided* that they recognize that the real issue and the most important issue is that they are sure they keep themselves under their designated *spiritual* authorities. Far too often, those who carefully observe the physical covering issue soon lose sight of the far more essential spiritual issue. This is vitally important to understand because of the angels or the spiritual forces involved here. "For this cause ought the woman to have power on her head because of the angels." (I Cor. 11:10.)

Many homes are suffering spiritual assault today because they have left themselves open to spiritual attack of these angels (fallen angels or spiritual beings) due to a misunderstanding of proper subjection to authority. Some wives and daughters face attack because they have never learned they should be under their husband's or father's spiritual protection, discernment, and authority. Others face attack because they have falsely assumed that their physical cloth covering is protecting them.

When I speak of spiritual attack, I am not necessarily saying that these wives or daughters are facing bizarre spiritual struggles or confrontations; often the spiritual attack here is subtle suggestions which come at these wives or daughters, similar to the spiritual attack Eve faced in the Garden before the fall. Spiritual attack often comes in the form of encouraging wrong reasoning in the minds of wives and daughters. This wrong reasoning in turn leads to wrong lifestyle or actions such as independence or authority usurping in subtle ways.

Many who believe that I Cor. 11:1-16 is discussing a physical (cloth) head covering claim that anyone who argues with their interpretation in this way is simply being "contentious". "But if any man seems to be contentious, we have no (other) such custom, neither the churches of God." (Verse 16.) In reality, the contentiousness in this passage is not over a cloth covering; but the concern is that the "head" or ultimate authority of the man remain Christ, not another man, and that the woman's (wives' and daughters') head remains her husband or father,

not another man. Paul states that there is no other teacher (himself included) in any of the churches that has a differing view to this authority structure as he describes it, and he urges the Corinthian believers to not be "contentious" over this arrangement of authority. The real and most important issue here is for wives and daughters to be certain they are living under the spiritual protection of their proper authorities. All wives and daughters need to discern this, both those who wear physical coverings and those who do not.

- What About Accountability -

Today we are hearing more and more teaching on this subject of accountability in the church. Actually one of the main objectives of accountability is a more intimate spiritual experience among believers. Our large assemblies today do not really allow opportunity for individual believers to open up their inner selves to each other. Smaller assemblies, in general, are an ideal atmosphere for this kind of intimacy where ladies can discuss appropriate concerns together, where men can discuss theirs, and where the church group, in general, has the freedom to acknowledge faults and pray for one another. I actually like the term "encourage-ability" more than accountability. Sometimes accountability borderlines on legality or can drift into legality and promote a falling away from grace. When we encourage one another, we put one another under grace. The early church met together to exhort, edify, and encourage one another; they were spurring one another on to Godly living. "Let us consider one another to provoke (spur on) unto love and good works." (Hebrews 10:24.)

In the early church, there was a sense of freedom in being able to appropriately "confess faults one to another and pray for one another." (James 5:16.) When we begin to hold one another accountable for certain Christian behavior, we tend to put each other under a legal system which in essence causes us to give greater regard to what our peers think of us instead of what God thinks of us. We tend to forget that we are, above all,

accountable to God for our Christian behavior. There are times when authority and accountability have been carried too far, times when God's people have allowed human authority to actually take the place of authority that God wants to have over their lives. This sometimes happens when God's people drift from wanting to be personally accountable and responsible to God for their actions, and they choose rather to be accountable to other men or the rules men have set up. One vivid illustration we find in Scripture of this occurred when the nation of Israel wanted a king like the surrounding nations around them. The account is recorded in I Samuel, Chapters 8–12. "Then all the elders of Israel gathered themselves together and came to Samuel unto Ramah and said unto him, Behold thou art old, and thy sons walk not in thy ways: now make us a king to judge us like all the nations." (I Sam. 8:4, 5.)

The children of Israel wanted to set a king over them to "fight their battles". They didn't want to be troubled with the concerns of warfare. So they assumed their king would do that for them. Today there are many Christian parents who do not want to take the effort to discern the spiritual warfare in their own lives or in the lives of their own children and homes; they want a king to tell them what to do and to give them the assurance that everything will turn out all right. Unfortunately many are sadly realizing under this system that everything hasn't turned out all right; and in addition, just as in the days of King Saul, their king has "taken your sons and appointed them for himself" and "taken your daughters" and so forth. (See I Sam. 8:10-22.) Samuel later pointed out to the people that had demanded for themselves a king that, "This day ye have rejected your God who Himself saved you out of all your adversities and your tribulations." (I Sam. 10:19.) The people had come to put their faith and confidence in the authority of their king rather than the Lord Himself. Now don't misunderstand, we need teachers, and we need to teach each other in the body of Christ, but we must be careful our teacher or leader doesn't become our king to follow.

In essence, remaining under or being accountable to a king is

like remaining a child. With maturity or growing up comes the obligation of being held accountable or responsible for our actions. There are a lot of Christians who just don't want to grow up because they don't want to be held accountable (to God) for their actions. There is a false comfort that comes with remaining a child; as long as we are doing what someone over us is telling us to do we think we're clear from personal accountability. However, in reality, we are going to be held accountable to God for the results of our life even if we let others make our decisions for us or tell us what to do. By being under someone who assures us of his wisdom or someone who is held in high esteem by many is not truly secure in itself. King Saul was a head taller than everyone else, but he was still far from being God Himself or a good leader to follow. It is usually harder to recognize our personal accountability when we have a false sense of security that comes with being under a notable authority or king or when we hold each other accountable for certain actions. A sometimes less recognizable type of kingship may come in the form of a denominational board or some other similar program with their mandates or decrees that can give us a false sense of security.

God intended for the church setting to be a place where one could go for encourage–ability, encouragement and direction in Godly, wholesome ways. Those in leadership were chosen because they were good examples to the flock, men with exemplary marriages and children. Those in the congregation looked up to and modeled their lives after these examples in leadership. Furthermore, each leader was a co–leader with other men of Godly character, and they encouraged and urged each other to maintain and live by Godly standards. Current teaching on accountability is simply an attempt to urge others to more righteous living through a pseudo–legal system (setting up a list of weekly requirements of each other, etc.). Actually God directed the apostles to set up Godly "examples to the flock" who could exemplify, teach, and encourage others in righteous ways. We will discover this early church system to be superior to modern accountability ideas. If the reader is involved in an

accountability arrangement of some kind, I would suggest to turn this into an encourage–ability session. This will put every-one under grace, and grace is ultimately far more effective in creating righteousness than the law or laws, and Christ will receive the glory.

Chapter Nine

The Spirit of Modesty in the Church

Springing up from the home schooling movement in recent years has been a new trend to return to modesty. I am seeing a concern among home schooling parents for modesty in the apparel they wear, the literature they read, the associations they make, the places they go, and the speaking they hear. I think this concern among home schooling families for modesty stems from two major reasons, the first being that parents are realizing that they fulfill an essential role of being the conscience for their children.

Children are not born with a conscience that clearly defines right and wrong in their minds. In general, children feel better about themselves when parents make them do what's right because a child who is left to determine this on their own will frequently choose wrong; and if this wrong is left unaffected by the parent, the child's conscience begins to accept this as right behavior.

The same is true in lifestyle presented to children through various media such as literature. For example, a girl who is

constantly reading about other girls who are away alone doing things or in other ways are acting independently (even for so-called good reasons) is being taught a subtle form of feminism, and your child's conscience will be trained to accept this as "normal" behavior for girls. Girls who are raised in a social atmosphere where they are encouraged to engage in regular social interaction and conversation with boys other than their brothers (or boys with girls other than their sisters), or where they are constantly reading passion novels where boy-girl relationships are the center of focus (or even lightly addressed or are an underlying theme) will grow to have a conscience that is unclear as to what is proper in this area.

And above all, parents are realizing that they cannot allow a society such as ours that has drifted dangerously far away from Biblical morality and modesty to dictate forms of modest apparel or anything else for that matter. So parents are realizing that shaping their child's conscience is an essential part of "training up" their children in the way they should go. A pure conscience in our children will lead to them having a pure lifestyle and motives.

Secondly, home schooling parents are the pioneers of new trends to return to modesty because through the home schooling movement they have already experienced to some degree what it means to be "peculiar" or different in their lifestyle. They have broken out of the mold and tasted the fruit of better ways for the home, and they are willing to continue this process in other areas of life such as modesty.

- Legal Codes Will Not Create True Modesty -

Modest apparel is frequently the outward manifestation of a heart that is seeking greater modesty and purity within. But outward apparel or appearance is not always a true indication of a desire for purity within. Sometimes outward appearance can be governed by decrees or regulations of those in leadership or by something that has been passed along as a matter of tradition or religious custom. In some cases, outward modesty

or reformation becomes a performance engaged in with hopes that this will create purity within; however many become disappointed with the results of this because this doesn't generally purify motives.

I have entitled this chapter "The Spirit of Modesty" because when modesty springs from within, generated by the Holy Spirit's drive for holiness in our life and coupled with a deep desire to live a life of purity that is pleasing to Christ, this is what will in time lead to a Christian having true outward modesty. When the purity comes from within, it is usually only a matter of time until the outward expresses the desire of the heart.

Jesus said to the Pharisees in Matthew 23:25, 26, "Woe unto you, scribes and Pharisees, hypocrites! for ye make clean the outside of the cup and of the platter, but within they are full of extortion and excess. Thou blind Pharisee, cleanse first that which is within the cup and platter, that the outside of them may be clean also." The Pharisees had extensive rules and codes for "looking" right, and I'm sure that they must have thought there was some kind of a medicinal affect in trying to look right outwardly; they probably thought that this would in time purify their motives and hearts. But Jesus said there is something very "blinding" about externals that have not sprung from a desire within (thou blind Pharisee), and this is very true. Often those who are careful to follow externals end up becoming unable to discern their own hearts clearly and accurately. Jesus said the best approach is to start searching and examining our motives and our hearts, seeking God's cleansing here first by grace, and this will motivate us to start making the necessary outward changes. The outward will then reflect a heart that is being purified by grace.

- Liberalism Will Not Allow Grace
To Create True Modesty -

Some Christians take the opposite extreme with modesty. They say since outward reformation does not guarantee inward

transformation we therefore need to take little or no concern for the externals. This isn't the correct approach either. Jesus said that the outward would become clean: "Cleanse first the inside of the cup that the outside may be clean also." There would be a resultant change in the outward by grace, but it wouldn't come about by following the decrees or mandates of religious regulations.

Those who hold we can do whatever we want often fall dangerously close to the world in modesty because they are not seeking true holiness. They, in a sense, "turn the grace of God" that is given to us to produce righteousness in our lives into a "license" to live pretty well however they feel or choose. A major problem with this way of thinking is that this license often surfaces in the form of excess rebellion or worldliness in their children and grandchildren.

Frequently those who have dabbled in excessive freedoms as a Christian begin to see discouraging character in their children's lives and in their home. Sometimes they attempt to remedy the problem by swinging over to a legal code and trying to live under a set of rules to remedy this. For years we have seen Christians drift more and more into extreme liberalism in lifestyle and dress. Many home schooling families are now reacting to this extreme liberalism and are swinging back to subtle legalism to balance this; but both of these extremes hinder the function of grace in the believer's life. The best road to follow and the only road that will yield true purity is that of grace coupled with the guidance of the Holy Spirit and wisdom. This will create a true sense of modesty in time. This is what I mean by the spirit of modesty. So now we see how modesty works in Biblical theory. How does it manifest itself in practical living?

- Listening To The Quiet Whispers Of Your Conscience -

Discernment of a true sense of modesty is not something that we achieve overnight. There is a process involved in coming to

understand a state of true modesty. As the process of sanctification takes place in our lives, our consciences become more sensitive to right and wrong, and things we allowed at one point will begin to bother us a few months or a year later. Growing sensitive to the small voice of our conscience is an essential part of Christian growth. Actually, many parents decide to home school primarily as a result of their conscience's reaction to what their children are having to cope with in a group school environment.

My wife and I saw this before we ever started home schooling when we were trying to send our little boys off years ago to toddlers' Sunday School class. We observed our young boys trying to cope with a lot of aggression and mischief, and they were picking up mannerisms that we knew we wouldn't allow at home. Other parents at church would remark with the old cliches of, "Oh, aren't they so cute?!", but we didn't feel it was so cute. We knew our children's attitude and conscience were being shaped by this interaction, and we didn't think it had to be a part of "growing up". This led us to realize when our children reached school age that this same set of circumstances would be presented to our children each school day to some degree.

For three years we sent our oldest child off to school and faced troubled hearts frequently over what he was facing, and my wife and I tried to ignore our consciences as best we could. We didn't know what to do. No one we knew was home schooling in those days, and, of course, we had lots of Christian friends who tried to assure us that the things we were seeing were normal or part of growing up and that "kids will be kids." We bought that reasoning for a while until our consciences matured to the point where we said, "We've had enough. We've got to do something."

Today we are being taught that the society around us is trying to dumb down the average American's intellect so that they can be manipulated and controlled. This is probably true; but a far more dangerous onslaught is the attempt we are seeing by those everywhere within the church and without who are trying to desensitize and dumb down our consciences as to what is right

and wrong, and what is modest. This is even more dangerous.

When we began home schooling and home churching, we were beginning to realize that we could listen to the sometimes quiet yet urgent cautions of our consciences, and through following the Lord's promptings be led to a state of feeling right about things in our life even if what we were doing was different. At that point in our Christian walk (about 17 years ago), Marge and I began discerning most every issue in life with a blended conscience as "heirs together" of the grace of life. By this I mean if Marge didn't feel right about something, I tried to respect how God's Spirit was working in her conscience. In the same way, she began to be willing to adapt herself to the feelings I had in my heart from God. We trusted that God was working in each of our hearts to guide us to His perfect will.

- Modesty In Dress -

One of the first areas in life we began looking at together was modesty. We took a comprehensive look at modesty. By this I mean we didn't just focus on apparel alone but also on actions, those with whom we associated, those from whom we learned, what we read about, and who we watched and admired. We began searching for that moderation that goes along with being a Christian. Gradually Marge and I both began to realize that longer dresses and looser fitting styles made with materials that didn't cling and weren't shiny or excessively revealing were more proper. The cotton, woolen, or linen type fabrics similar to those found in Bible times seem most appropriate.

Now that our daughters are getting older, they're making some of their clothes, although we do buy some of our clothing from clothing shops. When the children were little, Marge didn't have much time to sew. Marge feels that in Prov. 31, the virtuous woman had maidens, and a clothing shop that carries modest apparel can be a form of a maiden.

My wife began to wear her hair in such a way as to be simple, pleasant, and orderly, but not dowdy, nor fashionable or up with the latest styles. Both the Apostles Peter and Paul realized

108

that a woman's hair provides an excellent means for "professing Godliness" to the world around us. Therefore they both gave some directives on how the hair was to be worn. In both passages (I Tim. 2:9 and I Peter 3:3) the general description seems to go clearly along the lines that the hair was not to be elaborate in arrangement nor fashionable; neither was it to be neglected or unkempt in such a way as to distract from our message of Godliness. It should reveal our Christian moderation. My wife and daughters wear their hair long, and sometimes they wear it down and sometime they also wear it up. In I Cor. 11, Paul points out that even nature itself makes a woman feel right about long hair.

Make-up is something of moderation, too, and it will take time for some Christian wives to come to feel "right" about what is modest in this area. Those who try to be "legalistic" about this or hair styles will insist you're sinning if you wear any make-up or deviate from their prescribed hair requirements, but these same individuals will not think twice about going to the orthodontist or having a blemish removed; many times, they attempt to be as attractive as they can and still not break their "rules" in appearance, but often they break the rules in heart and motive. Some very light make-up may be acceptable for women professing Godliness.

The face and hair should comprise a woman's greatest attractiveness rather than trying to attract attention to their figure, legs, or feet. Modest shoes are also a consideration without wearing what the world around us calls unisex shoe styles that are worn by both men and women. Women's shoes should be feminine without attracting undo attention. "The woman shall not wear that which pertaineth unto a man, neither shall a man put on a woman's garment..." (Deut. 22:5.) God wanted women to look like women in their dress and hairstyles. They were to be feminine, not masculine in appearance. Some high heels and other revealing shoe styles seem inappropriate. Again, the face and countenance should be the point of attraction rather than the attire or form of a woman, being careful not to use excess make-up or jewelry. (My wife and daughters do not wear ear

rings or necklaces or bracelets, though they do wear modest watches sometimes.)

Many Christians feel that the wearing of modest wedding rings is important in showing ownership and is in keeping with the spirit of what Peter is saying in I Peter 3:3 (not wearing gold, etc.) and do not consider a modest wedding ring to be a form of jewelry. Those who have studied early church history know that Peter, Paul, the early apostles, and early church leaders did not set a legal system to dictate modesty. These early Christians were very familiar with the total inadequacy with such legal systems set up by the Pharisees and other religious leaders of their day.

Years ago as we began to grow in discerning modesty, some socially acceptable women's apparel began to becoming glaringly questionable. By this, I mean women's shorts, jeans, slacks, and as much as I fear to say swimming suits. Now we didn't question slacks quite as much as shorts, tennis suits, or swimming suits, but most women who are growing in Christian maturity will find their consciences to gradually speak to them over these things. We are certainly not trying to describe a legal system here either, and segregated swimming situations may be more tolerable for swimming lessons; but I cannot understand how Christians can speak in outrage against the immodesty in our world and then turn around the next day and have a Christian swimming party. It doesn't make sense to me.

I know some are trying to come up with modest swimming apparel (and this will be interesting to see), but we didn't quite know how to handle this. As our children were getting older, I wanted them to learn how to swim, but we didn't know what to do with the modesty issue. Since we live in Vermont where the summers are short and cool, about the time we thought about trying something with swimming, it would turn cool and soon fall was here. So we would put it off for the next year, and so on year after year, and as our children got older, they felt less and less comfortable with trying swimming attire. So our sons learned a little about swimming by wearing slacks and T-shirts, but our daughters have not experienced this. Actually, we do

not feel deprived in our lives in this area at all, and I recall that John Newton, the writer of "Amazing Grace", though a one time seaman, could not swim. He seemed to have a fairly fulfilled Christian life. Up until the 1930's and 40's, nearly every woman and most men got by in life without swimming; it seems to be a modern pastime that many are beginning to feel they can get by without. Many women have expressed the awkwardness with this issue to my wife and are finding comfort by our views in this area.

Years ago my wife and daughters began to feel uncomfortable with slacks. They used to wear them when ice skating and when out in the barn, but now they prefer wearing jean skirts; and if the weather is extremely cold, they wear woolen slacks underneath their skirts, similar to the idea of the old-fashioned pantaloons. Actually God intended for our homes to be the place to learn and exemplify true modesty. Modest actions and apparel, especially sleeping apparel, is very important in the home. Privacy is also important. Of course, ridding the home of immodest media is also essential. Purging the home of immodest books and magazines, radio, TV, and pictures all come into consideration here.

I want to clearly say that we are not trying to set a particular dress standard that everyone should follow. Let your conscience be your guide in this while remembering that the world around us has totally lost a sense of modesty, and be careful that your conscience isn't being molded or de-sensitized by exposure to the world's lower standards.

- Modesty of Actions and Motives -

In Genesis, Chapter 34, we find a story, an unpleasant story, of the dangers to God's people when they begin to drift too close to the world in appearance and actions. It is the account of Dinah, Jacob's daughter, and the defilement she faced at Shechem. Immediately following this chapter at the beginning of Chapter 35, Jacob at God's command decides to move away from Shechem back to Bethel. Jacob then commands his people to

do a few things. First, he told them to put away the strange gods; next, he required that they change the type of clothing they were wearing (I believe they had begun to wear the fashions of the Shechemites); then, Jacob buried their strange gods and gold earrings under an oak tree. Jacob knew they had drifted dangerously close to the Shechemites in appearance, jewelry, and idolatry, and he wanted to leave behind every trace of this.

However, when we go back to the beginning of the whole tragic episode, we find that they not only were looking like the Shechemites, but they began acquiring social interaction and ways similar to them. We see that because of their affinity with the Shechemites, Dinah felt a sense of freedom instead of caution in interacting with these idolatrous people. "Dinah, the daughter of Jacob, went out to visit the daughters of the land." (Genesis 34:1.) Once we begin looking like the world and enjoying its pastimes (idolatry), it becomes quite acceptable for us to act or live the way they do. We soon begin to acquire their lifestyle and ways, and often there is an immodesty in the things they do. So we must be discerning as to what is not only modest in appearance but also in action.

How can I be more specific without sounding legalistic? Here again with modest actions, there is a "spirit" of modesty. It would be unprofitable to specify modest actions without emphasizing the need to "feel" right about our activities. Again, our conscience needs to be very much a part of this. May I give some personal examples?

Years ago my wife began to feel uncomfortable being away from home alone, especially at night. Now you can't make a "rule" about this, but there is a sensing involved. We began trying to do things together, and if I wasn't available and it was essential for her to go somewhere during the day, she would take one of our older sons with her (this was good preparation for their future marriages). Sometimes it seemed okay for her to go with our daughters, but hardly ever alone. She began leaving the phone answering mostly to me or one of my sons (not one of my daughters). It was Jephthah's daughter in the

book of Judges who felt no reservation in going out the door. My wife began to acquire a shamefacedness in action instead of a bold outgoingness that we often hear praised as admirable character in younger women. She also began to feel improper in conversations of much length with other Christian men. We realize that the co-ed atmosphere of schools has contributed much to wives and daughters feeling okay in freedom of interaction and discussion with men; some of our present-day church practices have also encouraged this, but there also needs to be a properness in this area.

I also began to consider the modesty of my actions, and the modern work environment is making things more and more difficult in this area for men. I found it important to protect my wife from possible feelings of jealousy by avoiding situations that could have an appearance of evil. My wife and I have followed a general practice in counseling where I direct other women to her for counsel, and she directs men to me, or we will counsel others together. The church environment comes in again here, not only in interaction and conversation but also in holy (pure) greetings. The handshake generally seems to be proper (but not always) with those of the opposite gender, and we feel hugging should be left for those of the same gender in general. Here again, we don't want to set any hard, fast rules, but we should allow our consciences and feelings to guide us, and what seems okay at one point may be found to be inappropriate as time passes and as we become more sensitive in this area also.

- Modesty in Motives -

One final area that needs some discussion is the area of modest motives. Occasionally we hear of someone who faced an awkward situation, a troubling encounter, or something even worse like assault when it seems by all appearance that modesty was present in dress, and the actions did not seem that out of place. The root cause of this trouble is found in immodest motives. Outward actions and appearance can sometimes mask

impure motives and even give a false sense of security. Every Christian has the obligation to seek first the grace that cleanses that which is within and not try to cover this up. We do need to be careful with this topic. We can begin judging each other rather easily, labeling others as being impure in their motives.

The story of Boaz and Ruth when Naomi instructed Ruth to approach Boaz's sleeping mat at the threshing floor could have been considered quite improper. Why would Naomi encourage this? I think Naomi knew clearly that both Boaz and Ruth were very pure within (both Boaz and Ruth were very virtuous) and had good possession of their passions as well as pure motives of heart. However, even Boaz realized that this situation could have been wrongly construed; thus he sent Ruth away before it was very light in the morning. "Let it not be known that a woman came into the threshing floor." (Ruth 3:14.)

The Pharisees of Jesus' day would have no doubt quickly passed judgment on this situation, so there is a need to be careful with judging the motives of others when the appearance seems unusual. For example, the time when Mary anointed Jesus and held Him by the feet, or the situation with the woman at the well could have both been misinterpreted. There are times when the actions of those with pure hearts and motives are judged as wrong by those who have impure hearts. There are those who are very strict in outward appearance of modesty and are yet impure in their own motives, and they often become judgmental of others.

I hope this discussion has conveyed a call for us all to seek the true "spirit of modesty" in our lives, a spirit of modesty that gives us freedom from having to live by a list of rules but also a freedom that keeps us from making provision for the flesh through being too liberal in lifestyle. It has been a delight in recent months to see this grace produced moderation beginning to settle in the minds of so many of our home schooling family friends. Let us heed the admonition to "Let your moderation be known unto all men. The Lord is at hand." (Phil. 4:5.)

Chapter Ten
Are We Authorized?

As more and more smaller assemblies begin to be formed and established with the aim of preserving and enhancing the Godly home, we can be sure our adversary will attempt to slow down or stop this movement. When he sees new churches being formed that are just as zealous and active in evangelism as the "established" churches but who are also diligent in building up believers in Biblical truth while being careful to preserve and protect the sanctity and unity of each home present, he will become greatly alarmed. He wants to keep the status-quo of things going in our day because he knows the present system is not being overly successful in passing Godliness from one generation to the next. But whenever, in Scripture and Christian history, God's people are undertaking new directions or activities that will lead to righteousness and Godliness in their lives and in future generations, there are those who will attempt to keep things going as they are by accusing these Christians of being rebellious or unauthorized in their activities.

For example, when Ezra began to rebuild the temple in Jerusa-

lem to return God's people to a proper mode of worship that would have long range results, the adversaries of Judah and Benjamin began to "weaken the hands" of God's people through a letter campaign which basically accused them of rebellion and sedition. "Be it known unto the king, that the Jews which came up from thee to us are come unto Jerusalem, building the rebellious and the bad city..." (Ezra 4:12.) "This city is a rebellious city and hurtful unto kings, and that they have moved sedition." (Ezra 4:15.) Because of this false accusation, eventually the king sent a decree requiring the work to cease.

Later on when Nehemiah was involved in this work at Jerusalem, he was also accused of leading a rebellion by his activity. "It is reported among the nations, and Gashmu saith it, that thou and the Jews think to rebel: for which cause thou buildest the wall..." (Nehemiah 6:6.) Of course, none of these accusations were true, but this kind of opposition and reviling will always be experienced if what we are undertaking will lead to the good of God's people.

In the life of Christ and early apostles, we see many situations where the "authority" of Christ or the apostles was questioned by the "established" religion of their day. For example, in Acts, Chapter 4, we see this conflict. The rulers, elders, scribes, priests, and high priests all asked Peter and John, "By what power (authority), or by what name (authority), have ye done this (preaching)?" (Acts 4:7.) Basically, they were implying that Peter and John were unauthorized in this activity. To this, of course, Peter made his famous rebuttal, "We ought to obey God rather than men", implying that they didn't have man-ordained authority but that they did have direct commission from God for their activity.

Later on when the disciples were imprisoned for preaching the Gospel, Gamaliel pointed out to the religious leaders that if this ministry or movement is nothing more than other recent rebellions like the one led by Theudas or Judas of Galilee, then nothing will come of it. "But if it be of God, ye cannot overthrow it; lest haply ye be found even to fight against God." (See Acts 5:29-42.) Gamaliel recognized that there are times when God

moves directly with His people in some kind of God initiated and ordained activity or ministry. These same disciples later rejoiced that they had been "counted worthy to suffer shame or reproach for His name." Reproach is sometimes a part of starting something new.

This kind of reproach was a constant stigma of the Apostle Paul's life. Years later when he arrived in Jerusalem, one of the guards ignorantly suggested that the Apostle Paul was "...that Egyptian which before these days madest an uproar, and leddest out into the wilderness four thousand men that were murderers." (Acts 21:38.) The religious leaders accused the early apostles of teaching doctrine contrary to the Law of Moses and to the traditions of the elders.

So one can readily see that it's not going to be easy to start something new for the Lord's people without being labeled and falsely accused as rebellious. Furthermore, as the return of Christ draws closer, the "religious" fervor of the world will be heating up, and conflicts between religious groups, even true Christian groups, will grow. Those groups that stand for the greatest benefit of God's people and families will probably suffer the greatest reproach. They will be the ones who are "reproached for the name of Christ"; and any individual or group that is truly standing for righteousness and Godliness "shall suffer persecution".

Now, of course, we can be persecuted for being religiously lofty (prideful) or for having an unloving, rejecting attitude towards others who do not see things our way, and this is not true persecution; but there will always be persecution that arises from following truth. In Paul's ministry, he experienced the reproach and grief that comes with ministering the truth to Christians. Paul said to the Galatian church, "Have I become your enemy because I tell you the truth?" (Gal. 4:16.) Sometimes rejection comes in Christian circles because we are standing for the truth, or teaching ways that are more truthful. God sometimes begins to move in ways by His Spirit to bring about new Christian endeavors, and these movements are not always "approved" or "blessed" by other religious groups, particularly if

they run against the traditions.

- How Were New Testament Churches Started -

I think some insight can be gained by considering how some Christian works were established in the New Testament. Let's look first at the church in Jerusalem as described in Acts 4, 5, & 6. This church had grown to a sizable number of at least five thousand. In Acts, Chapter 6, they "looked out among them" and chose men of qualification ("honest report") to help participate in the ministry to this church. (Acts 6:3.) Then there is a persecution to arise after the martyring of Stephen; the Christians were scattered abroad, and many new Christian works sprang from this.

I would like to look at a few Christian works (churches) that became a result of this dispersal. The Scriptures say that the disciples "went everywhere, preaching the Word" (Acts 8:4), and we have some stories of some new converts like the Ethiopian and those in the villages of the Samaritans. We see the Holy Spirit was active in directing the course of these ministries. "Then the Spirit said unto Philip, Go near, and join thyself to this chariot." (Acts 8:29.) "The Spirit of the Lord caught away Philip." (Acts 8:39.)

We see similar direction of the Holy Spirit in the Apostle Paul's missionary works. "After they (Paul and those who were with him) were come to Mysia, they assayed to go into Bithynia; but the Spirit suffered them not." (Acts 16:7.) Actually when the Apostle Paul began his missionary work, "...the Holy Ghost said, Separate me Barnabas and Saul for the work whereunto I have called them." And the other disciples laid hands or agreed with the work they were undertaking. *But* they were "...sent forth by the Holy Ghost."

So we have two ministries going forth here—Philip, and all the disciples at Jerusalem who were sent forth as the result of persecution—and new works resulted from this. Eventually Philip has a church in his own home in Caesarea (See Acts 21:8), and he probably established other churches along his way. Philip

was not "authorized" by a church group to undertake establishing these new churches, but he acted in obedience to the greater authority of God's Spirit and direction in this service. In Paul's case, the Holy Spirit said, "Separate to me Paul and Barnabas." The direct ordaining of God's Spirit was responsible for initiating this ministry.

It was true that the other leaders in the Antioch church gave their blessing or felt right about what Paul was undertaking, but both he and Philip were directed through the Spirit's leading for their ministries. In Philip's case since he was one of the chosen "deacons" or leaders of the Jerusalem church, he was "qualified" to lead a church but was not directly commissioned or authorized to church planting by a parent church.

Actually the church that was at Antioch, where the disciples were first called Christians, was not established by any sort of authorized ministry from another church. "Now they which were scattered abroad upon the persecution that arose about Stephen travelled as far as Phenice and Cyprus and Antioch, preaching the Word to none but unto the Jews only. And some of them were men of Cyprus and Cyrene, which when they were come to Antioch, spoke unto the Grecians, preaching the Lord Jesus. And the hand of the Lord was with them; and a great number believed, and turned unto the Lord." (Acts 11:19, 20, 21.)

Here is a church that was first established purely on the Spirit's leading of some disciples from Cyprus and Cyrene. These men had neither commission nor authority from a parent church to start this work. Today some would argue that this church at Antioch would not be considered "established" under what they would consider as proper authority structure ways, but it certainly had God's blessing. Eventually this church was aided by the encouragement of Barnabas and then Paul. In house churches today and similar smaller assemblies, there is certainly nothing wrong with borrowing teachings from other knowledgeable and experienced Christians, but there is also nothing wrong with starting an assembly when it appears to be something the Lord is bringing about. This idea that churches have to be "authorized" by other established churches is not Biblically accurate.

Actually Christ's Great Commission is sufficient authorization for Christians to undertake new works and ministries, even starting new churches.

- Christian Movements in History -

Church history again gives us an untold number of incidences where "unauthorized" churches and ministries sprang as the result of the moving and anointing of God's Spirit. Today we are hearing teaching that the "established" churches in our land are somehow the "anointed" work of Christ, and new home churches or smaller assemblies do not share in this anointing. This is an error in interpretation.

The early reformers were men anointed of God who began to see the errors of the established church. These early reformers like Zwingli, Luther, and Huss were men of Spirit produced conviction whom God had ordained to be instruments of a beautiful transformation of Godliness in the church. At first, these men were warned for their "unruliness", and eventually they were hunted down and some even killed for their unswerving convictions; don't be afraid to face similar scoffing today. Some will argue that the reformers were contending with unbelievers and not true Christians, and among true believers we should not allow for divisions among Christian groups. We do not want to encourage a spirit of division among Christians, but neither do we want to share in other churches' errors. During The Great Awakening stirred up through the preaching of the Wesleys and Whitefield, these preachers soon found themselves excluded from Christian churches; many of these churches were operated by believing pastors and with congregations made up to a great extent of believers. As churches in our day drift more and more into worldliness and other practices which eventually cause problems in the lives of believers and families, something has to be done.

The Church of England had plenty of believers in it, and the Puritans tried to stay with it and purify it (and I'm sure this had somewhat of a seasoning effect on the established church). But

other men like William Brewster felt this was compromising, and they feared the impact it would have on their families. Similarly today many will not likely acknowledge home schooling parents as qualified, authorized, or even acceptable as teachers of our own children, and many of us pioneer home schooling families remember how uncooperative some of the Christian curriculum suppliers were years ago with us home schooling parents until the movement began to be more established. Church schools and Christian schools were their primary market, and at first they looked down at home schoolers until the merit of what we were doing became more apparent and our numbers increased. The same will be happening in this new church movement until the benefits of this kind of church environment for the Christian home become more apparent.

It always takes time for new works of God to get their roots established. Samuel was anointed as prophet, but it took time for him to become "established" as a prophet. Saul was anointed as king, but the people did not readily accept him as such at first. He was small in his own eyes in those days for a while. Solomon had to establish the kingdom in his hands. I would like to encourage families who are considering home churching not to become weary of this seemingly small work they feel the Lord is calling them to; it will, in time, prove very fruitful.

- What About Ordaining Elders/Leaders? -

In I Timothy 3 and Titus 1 & 2, we find a discussion of ordination requirements for those who would take a role of leadership in the church. Timothy and Titus were to go to their respective churches, take Paul's directives here described, evaluate the possible candidates, and then appoint them as leaders in the church. In I Timothy 3:1, we read a phrase that has some further bearing in the ordination process. Does the man "desire the office of a bishop"? This little phrase actually has to do with the moving or anointing process of the Holy Spirit involved.

Those who take a place of leadership should sense this presence of the Spirit urging and giving them the desire for the office

of a bishop; but then we have a whole list of character growth requirements that were to be fairly well fulfilled before the man should take the lead. So the man sensed the anointing or calling while also needing to prepare for the work ahead.

Timothy is no longer with us, but we still have the guidelines to follow to Biblically ordain someone into ministry. Today we generally give more emphasis to the ordination ceremony than we do either to the man's desire or anointing for the work, and seldom are his qualifications to do the job brought into the picture; and I have seldom heard of anyone being "unordained" as the Scriptures indicate if, in time, he "proved" inadequate for the task. "Let these also be proven." (I Tim. 3:10.) Some will contend that there is some kind of spiritual power passed on to an individual when he is ordained. This sounds good in theory, but this can often be only a mere mental exercise. Churches frequently "ordain" leaders when there is neither the desire, other than human desire rather than the God-generated, Holy Spirit's desire, for the office. D.L. Moody once said there are "too many man made ministers". Ordaining doesn't necessarily mean anointing, and I would question whether some ordinations are truly of God, having His blessing. I believe it is far more important today to be "Biblically ordained" by complying with the Scriptural guidelines than it is to go through some ceremony or service. The presence of an "official ordaining" is not really that valid in God's sight either.

I have met many fathers in recent months who have a desire to do a work for the Lord in this area of church assembly. They feel they have something beneficial to contribute to other Christians in the form of their spiritual gift and experiences, and they want to minister this. "As every man hath received the gift, even so minister the same one to another, as good stewards of the manifold grace of God." (I Peter 4:10.) They are not sent out by a mission board, commissioned by another church, nor have they graduated from a Bible school, but they sense a responsibility to minister their gift.

I believe God is not only placing this burden in their hearts, but He is arranging new church assemblies where this can be

possible. Let us not be intimidated by mis-taught authority teachings to think we are undertaking something that is not Biblical or in accordance with God's will. There will always be those, some who are even sincere yet misinformed, who will question things that look a little different from the traditional.

These new assemblies with their God anointed and Biblically ordained leaders will become an encouraging example for Christians today to return to some early church methods with its fruitfulness and wisdom. Don't let others detour you from this calling, but respond in obedience, and resolve to undertake this ministry. In some cases, it may be suitable and profitable to send out a "Timothy" or a "Titus" to a newly organized home group to help "set things in order and ordain elders". (Titus 1:5.) But keep in mind that we do have Paul's guidelines in making such determination for leadership, and individual groups can very readily make this evaluation on their own and designate or ordain their own leaders. Many groups today simply select their leaders in this way.

Just because your home church's name has not been around very long doesn't make it any less of a church assembly than those who are ordaining certain leaders for their known churches such as some Mennonite, Brethren, or Apostolic groups. Fortunately there is still not a list of state sanctioned churches today, and I know of many independent groups that have designated their leaders and filed their names with their county as ordained ministers of their particular group. This is quite acceptable policy, and the government recognizes these men as legitimate ministers. Christians that are "meeting together" may, in time, want to begin to designate or recognize certain men as the leaders in the group, and some kind of ordination ceremony may be appropriate at that point but is not necessarily required.

Chapter Eleven

Some General Considerations for the Church

- Child Discipline in the Church -

As parents begin opening up their homes for assembling with other families, and as other smaller church settings begin to arise, child behavior becomes an important issue. We know of one home church that eventually disbanded because one family's children were so disruptive. We feel that the church service ought to be a place where new babies and toddlers can be taken to regularly; but these little ones have the potential for disturbing the service, and parents should be sensitive to this. For this reason, a baby's church training ought to begin at home. That is where they need to learn to sit quietly for as long as Mother or Father wishes, where they learn to obey simple commands like "No", and where Mother or Father keep their word for discipline measures if baby disobeys these commands.

I suggest having family devotions a few times through the week with all the children present; don't put the little ones to sleep. Purposely make these home devotions lengthy at times, require the littles ones to sit quietly and obey simple commands

like "No" or "Shh," and don't allow the little children to get down or play. After a routine of this for a while, the children will learn to sit quietly. Of course, this practice at home will probably require some spankings, some corrective spankings, that are going to need to sting or smart a little if they are to be effective. You will find that you won't need to spank as much if you make the spanking hurt enough for the child to yield their will to your commands.

If your child does not yield to your words consistently, then you are probably not spanking firmly enough, and your child will grow to disrespect you as well as eventually other authority in their life. (For more information on the subject of child training, you may want to order a copy of our book, *Child Training and the Home School.*)

Some little children learn to try to be disobedient in social or public situations, thinking they can "get away" with it there. If the child is manifesting this during worship service and will not respond to your requests to be quiet, then he ought to be taken out and, in some room away from the audience, be corrected for this if this seems appropriate. If you find this to routinely be a problem then you are probably not attending to this enough at home.

Sometimes children who are removed from worship services for disobediance are allowed to run free or play somewhere else; this is a mistake in judgment. A child who thus gets his way will in all likelihood repeat this same performance the next service. Do not get into the habit of rewarding disobedience with liberty, but reward them with firm, loving discipline, and they will learn to respect you.

Again at the end of the worship service, parental restraint needs to be maintained with the children. Running, goofing, yelling, foolish talking, or other similar disorderly ways should not be permitted in connection with the worship service and the holiness of the fellowship (or any other time for that matter). Misbehavior among children is very contagious; if parents take the easy way and allow their children to run loose, they will be making it harder for those parents who are sincerely

trying to restrain their children.

We recommend keeping your children with you during Sunday worship service, sitting together as a family. Following the service, during fellowship time, we feel it is best to continue to keep your children with you under your supervision. As the men talk they can watch young boys, keeping them in order, holding their hands etc., or hold little babies for mother. As the ladies share together younger daughters should hold mother's hand or stay nearby. Many parents are diligently trying to keep their children in "subjection with all gravity" throughout the week, and much progress in this area of child order can be slowed down or hampered if we allow our children to frolic and be unmanaged during our home meetings. One newly formed house meeting we visited had a very proper worship service with children in order sitting with their parents. But following the service during the next several hours of fellowship time, the children were pretty much left to themselves, mothers becoming preoccupied with talking with each other and the men with the men. We felt the parents probably didn't need that much time together, and it would have been better for each family to go home after a shorter fellowship time and spend time with their individual families.

We found that having a meal time after the meeting each week to lead to discipline problems with children, also particularly if children are allowed to range freely in the homes. We began limiting our meals to once a month or even less frequently like once every couple months for this reason. I guess the frequency of time for meals together has a lot to do with how well the children are managed by each family involved. One family with very improper children will become a role model for all the other children and can make child rearing difficult for the other parents who are trying to do a good job with controlling their children.

Teen–age involvement is also a concern. If a sarcastic young man or an independent young lady is found to be a weekly companion of your teen, your teen may need counseling on how to cope with these or similar concerns. The fellowship time in home meetings needs to be wisely regulated; home churches

can present just as many struggles for our families as other church situations if child training is not a number one priority with each family involved.

Too many parents think that church is where our children are going to learn socialization skills, and a degree of this will be learned at church. But the real classroom of socialization is found in one's own home and depends on how well your children respond to you the parent and to each other, as brothers and sisters getting along.

Also bear in mind the frame of your little ones; church services of excessive length can make it difficult for them to sit quietly. We do not have Sunday School (most home schooling parents give adequate time to Bible study throughout the week), and little ones are cared for by parents or older siblings during services. A private area or room is provided for nursing mothers.

At this point we only meet together one day a week, but a mid week prayer/teaching time can be a consideration; however, be careful with too much involvement through the week. It can lead to social dependency and rob families of adequate routine family time needed to maintain family closeness. A meal about once a month seems to be about the most appropriate, and a men's meeting at this time would be helpful.

Meeting together once a week seemed to be the early churches' norm, but try to avoid making this a legal or expected obligation of each other. Allow God's Spirit to work in bringing you together with other Christians at the right time. There have been times in the summer when we have met with another family at a park or something similar for a time of worship on Sunday morning. God is not interested in seeing us follow a routine. He is much more interested in seeing our desire to meet together for the purpose of Godly edifying and holiness. The church should be a helpful extension of the family and become a support to our efforts to build a Godly home.

- Personal Evangelism and Family Ministries -

Today there is a missing element in the church that has great potential for not only reaching the lost world around us but also

the added dimension of being a vital part in discipling our own children; this missing element is the practice of personal evangelism and family ministries. The church assembly certainly plays a part in both evangelism and discipleship, but today Christians tend to over emphasize the churches' role in these areas to the exclusion of the dynamic potentials in personal and family ministry. Statistics show that the vast majority of Christians, 75-80%, have come to Christ through personal contact with other Christian friends or relatives. Most children come to Christ through the Christian influences in their own homes. Due to media coverage, most Christians think that large crusades and rallies are responsible for the majority of converts to Christ, when actually these kinds of evangelistic methods only account for a very small percentage of those who come to the faith.

A while back I started jotting down each time I had an opportunity to share my faith in a meaningful way with someone throughout the week. I kept a rather loose record of these times of personal evangelism, but I observed that in a year's period, I had shared Christ well over a hundred times. There were additional times when I just gave someone a piece of literature (a gospel of John, a N.T., a tract or booklet or cassette). The combined efforts of evangelism by other members in my family would push this number even higher.

Sharing Christ a hundred times in one year doesn't sound like a significant number, but if you had a church of a hundred members and each member gave this kind of attention to personal evangelism, in one year a small church of a hundred members would evangelize ten thousand individuals! A small home church of just a few families could very easily reach several thousand individuals with the Gospel. This kind of responsible evangelism year after year would reach tens if not hundreds of thousands of individuals in a meaningful one on one encounter in a relatively short period of time. It is rather easy to see how effective this kind of evangelism can be. I think this gives us some explanation as to why the house churches in such persecuting countries as China have been so effective in reaching the masses with the Gospel, as I noted in an earlier chapter.

The early church (for the first three centuries) relied heavily on the instrument of personal evangelism, and the greatest expansion the church has ever experienced in history was during those first three centuries. This is why our adversary would like to keep the potential of personal evangelism obscure today.

Several years ago America, and the world for that matter, was shocked by the incredible magnitude of the oil spill near Valdez, Alaska. The disaster occupied the front pages of the news for several months. I thought it was interesting to note that, as some research group pointed out, just single householders in America changing the oil of their own vehicles at home and disposing of it carelessly or improperly do the equivalent of *fourteen* Valdez oil spills in just *one* year! But it seldom reaches the headlines when an individual improperly disposes of his oil. Christians in America have a similar attraction to exalting the so-called big Gospel event or crusade, when many times they do not realize that by just playing a small part of a corporate effort they are actually exalting a far bigger event. This is why just starting a small, missionary, home church in some locality can grow to have great potential if members were encouraged with personal evangelism and ministry.

- Discipling Our Children -

There is an additional hidden element to personal evangelism and family ministry, and this is that it's a vital part to discipleship in the home. When children grow up in a home where they observe their parents regularly desiring to share their faith and minister to others, this becomes a tremendous role model for children to follow. This is one of the keys to discipling our own children. Today this evangelism is usually seen as a ministry of the pastor at a local church, and children fail to see their own fathers (and mothers) committed to this work. Children do not have the parental example to relate to, and so they, in general, lose interest and lack commitment to seeing in their own lives a potential ministry for Christ by copying the example of their parents. But, as more and more

home schooling families open up their homes for ministry, or in other ways develop family ministries, this will significantly increase the number of children and young people who are discipled by example and motivated to have or be a part of a ministry to others.

- Music in the Church -

Discerning proper music for the church setting usually requires time. Just as in every issue in life, tastes in music types change as our discernment grows. Generally we want a proper spirit to the tune, and we want a depth of wisdom in the lyrics of the music. Of course, we would recommend avoiding rock music and the contemporary rock type music arrangements. These types of music tend to "woo" the individual into an emotional high that then tend to cause them to crash into an emotional low. They also tend to give a spirit of confusion to the listener. Those who regularly listen to these types of music often face severe struggles and temptation in their moral life, as well.

Some who say they are against rock music actually often have a rock type rhythm in their music. Rock rhythm can often be conveyed through instruments other than drums (even a piano can be played with a hyper type of rock to it). Rhythmic clapping also conveys a rock beat. Be careful with all of these less recognizable types of rock music. The other extreme of music is your melancholy type music. This also plays on the emotions of an individual. This is the country type music, and there are a few old hymns that present this type of depressed style.

Of course, at times a sober, more minor keyed piece or hymn is appropriate for our spirits just as a cheery piece can sometimes lift our spirits a bit. But I would suggest avoiding continually playing, singing, or listening to music that plays on our emotions too much. An even keel in the emotions is best in sustaining an encouraged heart. Hymns that give an encouragement to our spirits without being overly emotional are the best, ones which have a nice melody with a wise and encouraging

message in the words. The tune will lift us up, and the words will sustain us.

We use *The Hymnal for Worship and Celebration* by Word Music. It's available through Christian bookstores and seems to have a lot of hymns that have good lyrics and tunes that are proper. As in most every hymnal, some arrangements may borderline on being too emotional or simplistic; others may be too minor keyed.

Evaluating your music together regularly will help the group to come to feel "right" about different hymns or songs they sing. Sometimes you will find that a particular piece or hymn that once seemed okay is beginning to bother your spirit a little, being too emotional, melancholy, or simplistic in style. Music plays a very important role in a Godly worshipful meeting. Seeking God's wisdom and discernment in this area should be a priority.

- Some Statements of Faith and Purpose -

I believe God is raising up families everywhere who have a vision for a Godly home, and they are looking for churches that will be an extension and support to these objectives. Many of these families would either like to start or be a part of an assembly which has a constitution, statement of faith, and more importantly a commitment to this end. The following list is a sample or suggested Statement of Faith and Purpose that the reader may want to use, all or in part, for their own home meeting. You may want to come up with a name for your home church; we've had different names for our home groups over the years such as Hope Fellowship, Grace Home Fellowship, etc. You many want to make up a handout that has your home church's name and a Statement of Faith and Purpose and objectives in it, and please feel free to use whatever you may want from this book, or use this book as a handout for those who may want to join you in fellowship.

1. The Bible being the inspired, infallible Word of God.
2. A statement concerning the Holy Trinity, Christ being the

sinless Son of God who came to pay the penalty for man's sin upon the cross, and His substitutionary death.

3. His bodily resurrection and His offer of the free gift of salvation through individual faith and acceptance of Christ as personal Savior.

4. Christ's soon return to gather His elect together into an everlasting kingdom.

5. The purpose of proclaiming the Gospel of Jesus Christ and of leading others to a personal relationship with Him.

6. The teaching of the Word of God for the building up of individual believers into a full maturity in Christ.

You may want to specify some clear objectives for your Home Church. May I suggest a few:

1. A clear emphasis towards holiness; holiness is a distant word in the vocabulary of most Christians today. There should be a return to true holiness.

2. A clear emphasis towards purity and pure speech which would include abstaining from references to the ungodly and perverse practices in the world around us. It would also include avoiding discussion which may provoke embarrassment or arouse the more tender consciences and minds of youth. All discussion of immorality or of adult content should be raised in private among appropriate mature adults. Public confession of personal sin or error should be avoided or expressed in general and unoffensive and nondescriptive terms. This would include testimonials, prayer requests, announcements, or other public discussions. Even some topics described in the Bible may need to be presented to the audience in such a way as to not be graphic or embarrassing in description. For example, one might say, "We now come to this distasteful story of David's sin....." The teaching should then be given in as modest of terms as possible without dwelling on the particulars involved, keeping the consciences of the audience in mind when discussing some of these morally descriptive passages. I believe God intended for discernment to be used in teaching these passages, and

some were probably meant to be read more in private. Moral issues described in the Bible should be presented with all purity. Concerning testimonies, instead of going into the details of a past sinful life or experience, it should be described in more general terms such as "I lived a shameful past," or, "I am sorry to say I lived a very ungodly life," etc. When the woman at the well expressed the details of her past sinful life, she didn't give a description to those in her city of any specifics but simply testified, "He told me all that ever I did." It was obvious from the context that she had lived a very sinful past, but she did not go into its details. Purity also requires a properness of conduct between couples, in general, with women conversing with women, and men with men. Greetings should be holy and pure. In general, any kissing or hugging should be between those of the same gender, and conversations should be kept on a surface level and brief between those of the opposite gender.

Purity of speech requires abstaining from referencing TV, movies, magazines, novels, videos, past experiences, sports or other illustrations that would tend to draw our minds towards worldly social practices or pastimes.

3. Modesty is more than having a proper outward appearance; it involves a modest heart and modest conduct too. Modest apparel for ladies would suggest the return to the long dress and other considerations which would be that of a "woman professing Godliness." Modesty of actions and properness of conversation between men and women falls under this category of modesty. Of course, modesty and properness of men's apparel should also be considered, and here again modesty in conversation, discussion, teaching or preaching should be carefully observed—giving consideration as to what would be proper topics for discussion in a holy assembly.

4. Meeting for the purpose of edifying. The church should meet together for the purpose of exhorting, comforting, and encouraging one another in Godly ways. Keep the time as a holy time, and be careful not to allow the meetings to lean too much towards socializing or play time.

5. Greater emphasis on the father's discipling their own fami-

lies rather than seeing the church as the sole instrument of discipleship, building up and encouraging fathers to take this role in the home. Men's meetings can play an important part in men encouraging and challenging other men in practical ways to disciple their own family by discussing marriage building principles and child training, discipleship concepts together.

6. A two fold goal in evangelism. We see evangelism in two streams. Of course, the more obvious is reaching out and evangelizing the lost degenerate world around us. Churches, in general, have focused their attention in this direction. But a less obvious and yet more important aspect to evangelism is encouraging each family in the church to responsibly and successfully help each of their children come to Christ and walk with Him. We have an alarming number of young people today raised in Christian homes walking away from the faith. One study put this statistic as high as seven out of ten young people raised in Christian homes turning their backs on Christianity. I believe having just one child walking away from the faith is too many; the church has performed rather poorly in this area of evangelism.

When Jesus said woe to those who cause one of these little ones who believes in Him to stumble or depart from the faith, I believe He was saying children will naturally believe and follow Him unless they are made to stumble at it somehow. Far too often today too much emphasis has been placed on evangelizing the world, and too little has been placed on helping our own children learn to walk with God. What does it profit a man if he gains the whole world and loses the souls of those dearest to him?—It will be very hard to bear.

7. What about Church membership? At this point we see no real necessity for having a church membership requirement for house churches. All of those who have believed in Christ have become a member of His body. I see no evidence of such a membership requirement for local churches in the New Testament. Certainly a "like mindedness" is of great concern to our Lord, and we should strive for this within our groups; and home schooling families, in general, already have somewhat of a basis

of unity in the area of family oriented lifestyle. We do not feel it is a good idea to be trying to "build" our organization by expecting some kind of a commitment from those who are presently involved. If this is truly a work for the Lord and by the Lord, He will keep it going by His Spirit.

- Church Division -

Another major area that has always been looked upon today with alarm is the idea of church division. Of course, church division arising from disputes within the church often causes bitterness and resentment, but healthy and natural church growth that may lead to starting a "sister" church in another location should be considered desirable. When a church group grows to the extent where it becomes impractical for most of the men to be able to exhort one another and minister their individual gift, then maybe it would be wise to consider starting another assembly. Communication with or attendance at different localities of home churches often give individual families an opportunity to visit a sister church to help break the routine of their regular church attendance. We do not feel some variances in church methods or doctrinal views or other differences need to become a divisional issue in fellowshipping in other church assemblies. In fact, such variances may even lead to one church learning from the experiences, theology, and practices of another. We have met few home schooling families who follow exactly the same curriculum program, but most of them we have met are doing a good job teaching their children. Perhaps we need to develop more tolerance among church group practices as well.

- A Network of Home Churches -

With the growing interest in the house church or other smaller assemblies, I can envision a network of such groups being formed in the future. If you are currently involved in such a smaller group or perhaps just have home church as an individual family and would feel free to give us your name or the

names and addresses of organizers, we would be glad to keep a list of such groups or homes so that we might make it available as a directory for inquiries we receive from different areas. We may be able to put you in touch with another family near your area that has similar goals and objectives in churching.

It appears from the New Testament letters that correspondence and intra-fellowship with other churches was a common practice in the early centuries. For example, Paul encouraged the churches of Laodicea and Colosse to exchange the letters they had received from him. There must have been freedom of intra-church relationships and perhaps mutual attendances. Some churches sent out elders to help newly organized churches get established in principle and doctrine to "set things in order". There certainly weren't the barriers we find today between churches.

- Home Church Network Affiliation -

We would not only like to have a directory of home churches but would also like to arrange for a non-commital association or affiliation of independent home churches. This would be similar to a denomination without the board or doctrinal control. It would be an association that tolerates some differences in convictions and interpretations (theology) among different autonomous groups, with our main coherence being that each group has the central theme and purpose of building and maintaining the Godly home as their foremost goal.

We could also offer teaching to fledgling home churches who feel they have not yet men fully qualified to head the group, and we also hope to arrange yearly or periodic meetings such as a camp meeting where various home groups could get together for fellowship, teaching, and sharing. Regional camps or a national convention or camp could also be a consideration.

If you would be interested in being a part of such an association, please fill out the enclosed registry form, and we will try to include you in our directory. If you have any questions or suggestions, pleae feel free to write or call us.

Conclusion

As can be seen, the home church offers a church setting that is more of an "intimate kind" where individual spiritual needs can more readily be ministered to. But along with this comes the problem of having to be more willing to tolerate deficiencies in each other's lives. In the bigger, denominational church one can go in, say "Hi" to someone else, and keep the level of communication on the surface. This is not as easy to do in the smaller assembly. Christian love, therefore, becomes more of a "must" in the smaller group, because love will cover the multitude of sin. Different families in the church will have different needs and weaknesses just as the individual children in one's own family. In the house church these needs and weaknesses will be more apparent. Patience and love are the Biblical terms that describe the necessary qualities for ministering to these needs and for tolerating the differences. The church should be a place where others can come and see examples of Godly homes and holy lives. This will not happen over night. It will take grace on God's part, and a willingness and diligence on ours.

Can we be of some assistance to you in this area of the church? Do you have a small group of a few families who would like some help in the areas of church leadership, child training, or similar family life concerns; OR are you a part of a larger existing church that could use some teaching on principles for the Godly home? We would like to make our ministry available to help and encourage you in these areas, and please feel free to contact us at *Parable Publishing House.*

The Apostle Paul's Charge to the Ephesian Elders from Acts 20:20 was:

"I kept back nothing that was profitable unto you, but have showed you, and have taught you publicly, and from house to house."